Other books by the author:

In English:

The Nine Pillars of History, a Guide for Peace

Radioisotopes and Circulation

Add Years to Your Life and Life to Your Years: Part I. Heart Attack Prevention

In Swedish:

Historiens Nio Grundstenar, Även en Guide till

Världsfred

Part II, Family and Work Enhancement

Add Years to Your Life and Life to Your Years

by

Gunnar G. Sevelius, M.D.

authorHOUSE®

AuthorHouse™
1663 Liberty Drive, Suite 200
Bloomington, IN 47403
www.authorhouse.com
Phone: 1-800-839-8640

First published by AuthorHouse 2/25/2008

ISBN: 978-1-4343-7343-4 (hc)
ISBN: 978-1-4343-5535-5 (sc)

Library of Congress Control Number: 2007909910

Printed in the United States of America
Bloomington, Indiana

This book is printed on acid-free paper.

The eternal loop pictured on the cover is an old Chinese sign for longevity.

In the *Annals of Internal Medicine* 12:964, 1939 George M. Piersol and Edward L. Bortz said: The society which fosters research to save human life cannot escape responsibility for the life thus extended. It is for science not only to add years to life, but more important, to add life to the years.

DEDICATION

Part II is dedicated to the Management of Lockheed Missile and Space Company. At the time it was pioneering to support an employee health education program.

ABOUT THE AUTHORS...

In Regard to Headache

Helen Goodell was Research Associate of Harold Wolff at Cornell-New York Hospital for 30 years and as such participated in his studies of headache. Following his death in 1962, she readied the manuscript of the second edition of the monumental "Headache and Other Head Pain" for publication by the Oxford University Press. Her article entitled "Thirty Years of Headache Research in the Laboratory of the Late Harold G. Wolff" is a summary of Harold Wolff's work and prompted invitations to her to lecture on this topic in Boston, New York, New Jersey, Australia, India, Turkey, Sweden, and South Africa. Although retired for several years, she continues to work with and to give editorial assistance to Dr. Stewart Wolf.

Stewart Wolf, M.D. was Professor of Medicine at Temple University in Philadelphia, Pennsylvania and Director of the Totts Gap Medical Research Laboratories, began his career at the Johns Hopkins Medical School and later worked for 14 years at Cornell-New York Hospital in New York City as a Resident, Fellow and colleague of Harold G. Wolff. Subsequently, Stewart Wolf had professorships in medicine, physiology, neurology and psychiatry at the Universities of Oklahoma and Texas. He was awarded an Honorary Doctorate from the University of Göteborg, Sweden. His research has been and continues to be focused on psychosocial and neural influences in health and disease.

In Regard to Family Social Support

John G. Bruhn, Ph.D., Dean of The School of Allied Health Sciences, Special Assistant to the President for Community Affairs, and Professor of Preventive Medicine and Community Health at The University of Texas Medical Branch at Galveston, and Professor of Preventive Medicine and Community Health at the University of Texas School of Public Health in Houston.

He is author of numerous scientific articles and co-author of many books.

We would like to thank Mrs. Paula L. Levine for her help in gathering, reviewing literature and editing the text in the chapter on Family Social Support and we are grateful for the professional work of Ms. Shane Tout who contributed the sketches.

In Regard to Drug Basics

Modern medical science can be divided into two major efforts: to treat and to educate. Because most diseases nowadays are due to behavioral diseases, public education has become a major part. Wesley Alles, Ph.D. recognized this need early and is therefore Part I and II are dedicated to him.

Ed Brandt Jr., M.D., Ph.D. was Assistant Secretary of Health from 1981-84 and U.S. representative to the executive board of the World Health Organization. Ed Brandt established the first Public Health Service Task Force on Women's Health. He is past Dean of Oklahoma University College of Medicine and has, since 2005, taken the status of Regent Professor Emeritus.

In Regard to Alcohol

I want to express special thanks to my old friend, A.J. "Sully" Sullivan. Sully, an executive engineer at Standard Oil of California, who has had more experience with alcohol and its treatment than most. He successfully recovered from the ill effects of the disease some 22 years ago and has since dedicated his life to working with more than 4,000 affected people. Sully started the Employee's Assistance Program at Standard Oil that, through its success, has become a model for similar programs in other companies, including Lockheed. Sully was one of the 11 founders and the second president of ALMACA (Association of Labor, Management, and Consultants on Alcoholism).

Special thanks are also given to Gary Atkins, LMSC Employee Assistance Program coordinator and alcoholism counselor. His contribution of time and effort is greatly appreciated.

The same team that was so successful in developing the Heart Attack Prevention series is still with me. This ensures success. The staff in technical publications has given me their gifts of talent and expertise in publishing this text, and of course, nothing would have been done without my secretary, Gloria Braman.

In Regard to Aids and HIV

Donald I. Abrams, M.D. graduated from Stanford Medical School in 1977 and is a Diplomate of American Board of Internal Medicine and also in the subspecialty of medical oncology. Dr Abrams was the first doctor to draw attention to an unusual frequency of Kaposi's sarcoma in young males, leading to the ultimate recognition of AIDS and HIV. Dr. Abrams is Professor, Clinical Medicine, UCSF; Chief, Hematology-Oncology, San Francisco General Hospital; and Director of Clinical Programs, Osher Center for Integrative Medicine.

Since his first involvement with the AIDS epidemic in San Francisco, Dr. Abrams has authored or co-authored many scientific reports and reviews about the HIV disease. Thanks to the input from Dr. Abrams, Lockheed Corporation was the first company to hire and to cover HIV-infected people under its employee health insurance.

In Regard to Dental Health

John W. Goodhart, R.D.H. has a Master's Degree in Public Health, specializing in health promotion and occupational health education. He is also a fellow of the Society of Public Health Educators. John did his postgraduate work at our Medical Department.

Samuel Wycoff, D.M.D., M.P.H., Professor of Preventive Dentistry and Community Health and Chaired the Department of Dental Public Health and Hygiene at the University of California, San Francisco, California.

In Regard to Back Care

Professor Alf Nachemson of Göteborg, Sweden and his co-workers clarified the biomechanics of the spine by measuring the actual pressures in the discs when the body is in different positions. This pioneering work has contributed to the present understanding of backache. I am grateful that Alf took time out from his busy schedule to review, suggest improvements, and approve the manuscript for publication.

I would also like to acknowledge Dr. David A. Thompson, Professor of Industrial Engineering at Stanford University. His 27 years of experience in industrial ergonomics was an invaluable resource in formulating the chapter on Back Care.

In Regard to Noise and Hearing Conservation

For this chapter I am particularly indebted to Alice Suter, Ph.D., Adjunct Professor of Audiology and consultant in hearing conservation in Silver Spring, Maryland. Dr. Suter is the principal author of the present OSHA hearing conservation standard. Dr. Suter has reviewed the text and has edited it so that it complies with the spirit of the law. I hope that this text will help you protect your hearing for many years of "sound" enjoyment.

I also wish to express my gratitude for constructive suggestions from Vern Glick, Director of Manufacturing in the Lockheed Space Systems Division; George Tomer, Manager of LMSC Industrial Hazard Control & Emergency Services, and staff, who are responsible for administering the Hearing Conservation Program at LMSC; and Ted Raia, Missiles Systems Division, Representative for Industrial Safety.

In addition, I am grateful to Carola Rudd who, as an intern in health education, performed the literature search; to my secretary, Gloria Braman, for coordinating the project; and to ASD Technical Publications for their assistance in producing this text.

Finally

I wish to thank Cheryl Cooper and Wendi Freeman, who have painstakingly transformed all the text and pictures into digitized format.

Gunnar G. Sevelius, M.D.

Contents

PREFACE

This is a series addressing family and work life. My goal is to restore the support and enrichment family and work can give us. I hope this series will be as well received and successfully consumed as the series on heart attack prevention.

Some 70-80 percent of all diseases are rooted in our habits and are preventable. Having easy access to information about how to prevent disease will give each one of us a chance at a longer and happier life. It would also be appropriate here to express our thankfulness to the Lockheed Corporation, which has pioneered and partly supported this effort for their own employees. It is an effort that has benefitted both the corporation and its workers and is widely praised as exemplary.

HEADACHE

Helen Goodell

Stewart Wolf, M.D.

When the head aches, all the body is the worse.

English Proverb

INTRODUCTION

Have you ever had a headache? If you can honestly answer "No," then you are one out of only 15 percent of all the people in the United States who have never had a headache. The fact that you are reading this book means that you probably belong to the nearly 200 million people in the U.S. (the other 85 percent of the population) who have suffered from a headache at one time or another.

The headache is one of the most common complaints of civilization. Without discrimination, it strikes young and old, male and female, rich and poor, city dwellers and farm workers, in every nation of the world. The occasional headaches that most of us suffer cause little inconvenience and are easily controlled with simple over-the-counter medications. When frequent or persistent, however, headaches can pose a real handicap.

THE NATURE OF PAIN

Although man has been concerned with pain since the dawn of time, it was not until the last century that pain was even recognized as a sensation. Almost 2,400 years ago, Aristotle advanced the doctrine of the five senses: vision, hearing, taste, smell, and touch—but not pain. Even though the ancients certainly experienced pain, they regarded it as a "passion of the soul." They thought of pain as the direct opposite of pleasure, rather than as a specific sensation.

Not all pains are necessarily unpleasant. The mild burning produced by putting iodine on a cut is considered by some to be an agreeable sensation of "clean healing." In certain religious rites and sexual practices, pain is associated with a feeling of exultation. For most of us, however, pain is unpleasant.

An emotional or physical response to the unpleasant aspect of pain is classified as a *pain reaction,* in contrast to *pain perception,* which designates the recognition of pain as a sensation different from all other sensory experiences. In other words, *pain perception* is what you feel and identify as a distinct sensation; *pain reaction,* expressed through sweating, groaning, etc., reflects the anguish or unpleasant aspect of pain.

THE PAIN OF HEADACHE. In the broadest sense, headache means any pain in the head. Most headaches don't require medical attention because they are not frequent or severe. In fact, only about 10 percent of the people who have headaches suffer from intense and/or frequently recurring pain. Why is it, then, that even a mild headache often causes concern which is all out of proportion to the intensity of the pain?

When pains of nearly identical intensity are induced in various parts of the body, the greatest pain reaction is observed when the pain stimulus involves nerves that supply the head and mid-chest. Without doubt, pain in the head or near the heart causes exaggerated anxiety because the head and the heart, compared with other parts of the body, are so important to the person.

The intensity or frequency of a headache does not indicate its cause or significance. The most life-threatening diseases may be associated with mild headaches; on the other hand, a person in good health may suffer from headaches that are severe and that recur frequently. Intense and frequent headaches may cause much misery, but they seldom indicate a serious underlying condition as their cause. Nevertheless, most people with intense or recurrent headaches worry about the possibility of brain tumor.

When told by their doctor that there is nothing really wrong, many patients worry that not enough tests have been performed to rule out brain tumor. But, the statistics are favorable. The chances are 199 to less than 1 that even a severe headache is due to a tumor. These statistics, however, fail to comfort the anxious patient unless the doctor can give firm assurance that he is not that 1 in 200. Fortunately, today a physician can rule out the possibility of brain tumor with reasonable accuracy by brain scan and other modern diagnostic techniques.

It is common for patients, parents, friendly neighbors, or even physicians to attribute recurrent headaches to eye, sinus, or tooth problems. While pain in the face or head may arise from disturbances in these structures, they are only rarely the source of recurrent headaches. Many sinuses have been probed and healthy sets of teeth extracted only to have the headache persist. A careful and convincing medical or dental evaluation is required before the headache can be blamed on the eyes, nose, teeth or jaws.

Until the work of Harold Wolff and Associates, very little was known about the mechanisms for headache. Yet headaches have plagued humans since our earliest days, and we have long exercised our ingenuity in devising ways to cope with headaches—even going to the extreme of boring holes in a victim's head! Present-day methods of dealing with headache depend upon a better and more recent understanding of pain and of headache mechanisms.

PAIN MECHANISMS. There are two types of muscle contraction that can produce pain: sudden, powerful contractions; and sustained contractions of moderate degree. The first type produces the pain associated with a "Charley horse" or bone fractures, but usually is not the cause of headache; most headaches stem from the second type, sustained, but less intense muscle contraction.

Pain results from the accumulation of waste products that irritate pain nerve endings. There is an associated constriction of blood vessels that slows the normal flushing out of waste products from the local tissues, thereby causing pain to persist.

A helpful way to counteract this process is massage and application of heat, especially hot, wet towels, or a steaming hot bath with the head resting against a folded towel and the ears just above water level. Relaxing the muscles in such a manner permits the blood vessels to expand. Blood flow is thus increased, the waste products are flushed out, and the pain is relieved.

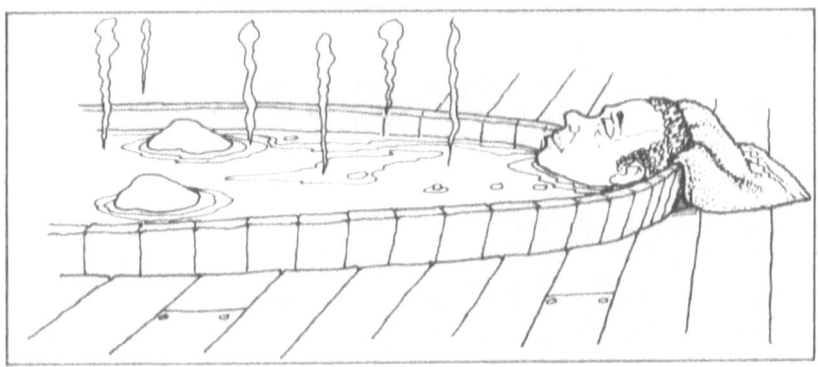

HEADACHE FROM PAIN IN MUSCLES

SITUATIONS AS SOURCE OF MUSCLE HEADACHE. When a situation is the source of a headache it is often called a situational or tension headache. Tension headaches are not usually intense, but are often persistent. A muscle tension headache does not necessarily begin with a pain in the head. The first sign of an impending headache may be stiffness and soreness in the back and shoulders, followed by the sensation of a tight band around the head. Sometimes hard and tender lumps (or "tight cords") can be felt in the neck and shoulder muscles.

Patients with a tension headache are usually most comfortable sitting up, with the head leaning forward and supported by the hands. They often find it difficult to open their mouth wide because of jaw muscle contraction. Massage of the body or neck may ease the pain intensity; exposure to cold with shivering, however, may make the pain more intense.

Medical examination usually reveals tight muscles and areas of tenderness. Pressure on the tender areas may produce or accentuate the headache and may cause the pain to spread to other parts of the head. The pain may last for a short time or may persist for days, weeks, months, or rarely even years. When the headache is persistent, it is usually accompanied by fatigue; in fact, the patient may wake up in the morning feeling tired.

By far, the largest number of muscle tension headaches occur as part of a healthy person's attempts to cope with the challenges and frustra-tions of daily living. Consider this, for example: You're a businessman who has had a hectic week at the office. On top of that, you've spent every evening working on your income tax report. Then you discover a mistake that throws off all of your computations. Your head aches; the muscles in the back of your neck and across your shoulders are tight and sore. You have a muscle tension headache.

Or this example: You are a parent whose teenage son wants to drop out of school. Your ten-year-old daughter has the measles, and the twins, home from school with coughs and fever, are fighting and screaming at each other. All morning you have felt as if you had a tight band around your head; your scalp is taut and sore all over, and your head feels heavy. You're afraid you may have something serious and wonder how your family can get along without you. You have a muscle tension headache.

Perhaps while driving home on a Sunday afternoon, you find yourself creeping slowly behind a long line of cars. To make matters worse, your guests in the car keep reminding you that they have to be home at a certain time, and your spouse helpfully adds, "I told you we should have gone the other way!" You're hot, tired, exasperated—and your head aches.

Or you may be a 34-year-old factory worker with a pain mostly in the back of your head that feels like someone socked you. Sometimes the pain spreads all over your head and into your right shoulder and arm. You have stomach trouble, you've been getting more and more absent minded, and you feel "down in the dumps" and discouraged most of the time. You hate to get out of bed in the morning and you've been late for work more than once. Such feelings of depression and often of guilt frequently underlie tension headaches that persist more or less continuously.

The circumstances that precipitated the headache may not have been recognized—in fact, the person may not even be aware that he/she is depressed. The individual may show little evidence of emotional disturbance and blame the headache on his/her constant weariness and lack of enthusiasm. Other symptoms of depression may be dryness of the mouth, poor appetite, and difficulty sleeping, with frequent early morning wakening.

When headache is associated with deep discouragement, the most fundamental approach is effective management of the patient and of the depression. Useful as they are for the occasional muscle tension headache, pain relievers offer little for the victim of chronic tension headache. Even a tranquilizer or "energizer" drug can provide only brief, pain-free periods; the headache will keep coming back until the underlying problem is identified and dealt with (a task that has become too much for the patient to handle; an interpersonal relationship that has gone sour, the support of a loved one that has been withdrawn, or frustrating circumstances that must be endured.) The headaches may then yield to discussions with a skilled physician who offers understanding, encouragement, counseling and other measures.

WHAT YOU CAN DO ABOUT YOUR SITUATIONAL HEADACHE. The vast majority of tension headaches are not of serious concern. The occasional tension headache experienced by most of us can usually be quickly dispelled by simple headache remedies such as aspirin (acetyl salicylic acid) which has been the standard non-narcotic, non-prescription pain reliever since its discovery by Bayer in Germany near the beginning of the 1900s. Since then, several substitutes for aspirin have been introduced.

Nearly every drug with beneficial effects has potential toxic effects as well. Aspirin, for example, a generally well-tolerated drug can cause stomach irritation and bleeding, even serious bleeding in a few people. Efforts to reduce the likelihood of bleeding have consisted mainly of combining an alkali with aspirin as in the case of Bufferin or Ascriptin. Another device has been to coat the aspirin with a material that enables it to pass through the stomach and to be absorbed in the small intestines. Acetaminophen, the ingredient in Datril and Tylenol has not been found to cause stomach bleeding but in large doses has been implicated in liver damage. Naproxen or Aleve, another popular pain reliever (non-steroid anti-inflammatory drug or NSAID) may cause stomach bleeding or liver damage but is safe for most people. Moreover while its actions in the body are, to a large degree similar to those of aspirin.

Ibuprofen, the active ingredient in Advil and Nuprin, is generally well tolerated but can be toxic to some patients. Experience with ibuprofen for headache also is relatively short. There is no clear-cut evidence that any of these agents taken in safe quantities is superior to another in its ability to relieve pain.

All of these remedies relieve only the symptoms, but not the cause of headache. When your tension headaches occur frequently and are seriously troublesome you may be able to alleviate them by a little self-study and perhaps by modifying your attitudes or circumstances.

If you have some insight into the reasons for your headache, you may be able to find relief by changing some of your activities. It may be possible for you to cut down on your outside responsibilities, work less at night, or change your home or your job. Maybe you need a vacation, or a new interest or hobby. A long, honest talk with your boss or a relative might smooth out a tense relationship and help reduce some of the pressure on you.

Of course, some situations and people can't be changed. And sometimes changing your residence, your job, or even your lifestyle may fail to eliminate the headaches. In such a case, it is important that you look within yourself.

What are your goals, your values? What do you really want to get out of life, what do you hope to accomplish? The answers may surprise you, and they are fundamental to any effective attempt to adjust your way of life into a healthy, satisfying, rewarding direction that will lead to freedom from headaches.

You may be able to learn more about yourself by talking to someone close to you. Such communi-cation can often provide support, reassurance, and encouragement that you may desperately need without realizing it. You may begin to open up, to realize that some of your fears are not so terrifying after all, to rid yourself of some of your guilt feelings, and to discover new ways of coping with your problems. As our self-perception becomes more realistic, we may try to find new satisfactions and to strengthen our commitments and our relationships. When we do, the world may begin to look brighter, friendlier. As you begin to enjoy what you're doing and begin to feel more adequate as a person, your headaches may become less and less frequent until, eventually, they become a thing of the past.

To start this process of self-reappraisal, it is often helpful to do so under the guidance of an interested physician. He/she may recommend that you list your earliest ambitions, then indicate what has happened to each one and why. It is also helpful to list what you consider to be important life goals for every man or woman and what qualities in people you find admirable. Then perhaps you can look realistically at the qualities and characteristics of your family members, your boss, your friends, and other associates.

Although you may be surprised at what turns up, the information will probably be useful to you in your reassessment and in shaping changes in your future behavior.

Usually it is not necessary to make any great changes in your pattern of life; a small shift in emphasis, a reordering of priorities, just gaining perspective, an understanding of yourself and of your relation to other people, may be enough to ease the burden of headaches.

For completeness we want to mention that tightness of muscles around the head may rarely be a symptom of inflammatory reactions such as sinusitis or meningitis. The teeth and eyes also may be occasional sources of muscle tightness.

TEETH AS A SOURCE OF MUSCLE PAIN. There seem to be many ways that tooth trouble can cause head pain. In the case of an apical abscess or other acute infectious process, attention is usually called to the teeth by visible facial swelling, and soreness of the gums and the lymph nodes under the lower jaw. A less acute type of infection around a tooth, an apical (around the root) abscess may produce headache but not swelling of the face.

Other causes of tooth and jaw pain are not as readily apparent and are poorly understood. The balance of the lower jaw and evenness of the bite appear to be relevant. Improper *occlusion* may cause muscle contractions that result in pain radiating into the face, ears, head, and/or neck, often at some distance from the teeth themselves. There may even be soreness at the back of the throat. Such disturbances in jaw alignment and the resulting strain from chewing and biting also seem to precipitate headaches of vascular origin, especially in the lower branches of the external *carotid artery* (the artery felt pulsating just behind the angle of your jaw). However, lower-half headache as it is called, may occur independently of tooth trouble or jaw misalignment.

Inflammatory reactions may be set up in the tooth pulp or in the gums by various injuries. (See Dental Health). An unbalanced bite may result from the removal of a tooth, from food or other foreign matter between the teeth, or the pull of corrective braces. Occasionally, a patient exhibits bruxism, grinding of teeth and clenching of jaws excessively, especially during sleep. The result may be pain in the temples, which radiates upward, backward, and forward because of the constant tension of the muscles of the head, neck, and scalp.

Costen's syndrome, familiar to many dentists, refers specifically to those pains arising from asymmetry of the bite and hence movement of the jaws. The pain was formerly thought to originate from the temporomandibular joint (the hinged joint of the jaw), but is now generally acknowledged to derive from the muscles that move and stabilize the jaw, and may spread over a large area. Such headache, usually accentuated by yawning, chewing, and swallowing, is particularly common in middle and late life, occurring especially in those who have lost some or all of their teeth. Another cause of face and head pain familiar to dentists is the increased sensitivity of a nerve that has been damaged but not completely destroyed.

EYES AS A SOURCE OF MUSCLE PAIN. Rarely can headaches in and about the eyes be traced to the eyes themselves. Although headaches due to eye disorders are rare, they can be intense and their implications may be ominous. One of the most serious headaches involving the eye is *glaucoma.* In glaucoma, the pressure within the eyeball is raised by a restrained fluid flow inside the eyeball. When the pressure is high enough or long-lasting enough to damage the optic (eye) nerve as it enters the eyeball from behind, blindness may result. In glaucoma, the pain may be felt directly in either or both eyeballs. The earliest visual disturbance is usually the appearance of halos, sometimes in color, around any source of light at which the patient looks.

Other very intense headaches from the eye can be caused by scratches or ulcers on the *cornea,* the clear surface of the eye or by inflammation of the iris, the muscle ring around the pupil which gives eyes their color.

The most common headaches attributable to eye trouble are related to farsightedness, astigmatism, and, especially, misalignment manifested by strabismus (cross-eyes or wall-eyes.) Efforts to compensate for these handicaps by contracting the intrinsic eye muscles that control the thickness of the lens and the extrinsic muscles that move the eyes are of little avail and often lead to further sustained contractions of the neck and scalp muscles and a typical muscle tension headache.

The treatment of "eye headache" depends on the mechanism responsible for the pain. When pain is due to glaucoma, the fluid flow in the eye must be controlled to ease the pain and protect the sight. When an infection of the iris or another part of the eye is responsible, the infection must be treated to relieve the headache. When the trouble is in the muscles of *accommodation,* corrective glasses are the proper form of treatment.

HEADACHE FROM PAIN IN BLOOD VESSELS

MIGRAINE HEADACHE. Migraine is a vascular headache that comes mainly from those blood vessels in the head that are outside of the skull. The word migraine means one-sided, and indeed most migraines hurt on one side of the head, at least at the beginning, and later the whole head may be involved.

Migraine, a very common headache, was distin-guished from the general group of headaches at the end of the first century AD by Aretaeus of Cappadocia (a physician in ancient Italy). He noted its paroxysmal nature, its severity, its one-sidedness, and its association with nausea. He also observed that, between severe bouts of pounding headaches, the patient may be altogether free from discomfort; indeed, he may have a feeling of unusual well-being.

A migraine attack may last from a few minutes to several weeks, but most often it lasts only one day from "sun-up to sundown" with relief occurring during the early evening. Preceding a headache there may be mood changes, including irritability, apathy, or a sense of unusual buoyancy. An occasional patient may experience dizziness or strange sensations in one arm. More commonly, there may be disturbances of vision, such as spots before the eyes or jagged lines or flashes of light, which last from a few minutes to an hour or more before the headache starts. There may be small, scattered blind areas or temporary blacking out of a large portion of the visual field in one or both eyes. These distressing happenings are due to a brief constriction of arteries in the retinas or behind them in the part of the brain concerned with vision. As the headache begins, the visual disturbances clear up as the constriction of the arteries gives way to wide dilation or expansion.

There is more to the migraine attack than the headache. The migraine attack is a widespread disorder accompanied by disturbances in many systems of the body. Not only nausea and vomiting but diarrhea or constipation may accompany the pain. Breaks in the rhythm of the heart, felt as palpitations, are common. The liver may provide the products of fat metabolism to be burned by the muscles in preference to sugar (glucose); the *adrenal glands* may secrete expansively, and the usual balance of water and salt content in the body may be upset. The adrenals are two small glands located one on top of each kidney. Each gland consists of two parts: the inner part, *medulla,* supports short time stress by secreting adrenaline into the blood stream; the outer part, *cortex,* supports long term stress by secreting cortisone like substances and by controlling water and salt metabolism. Some patients may store water in their tissues so that they gain as much as nine pounds immediately before or during a headache. The feet may swell so that shoes do not fit, or the fingers may swell so that rings cannot be removed. As the headache subsides, enormous quantities of urine may be passed with the result that the extra body weight is lost.

Pain Mechanisms of Migraine Headache. As with all vascular headaches, the pain of migraine depends on the network of nerves in the walls of the arteries. When an artery is relatively expanded or dilated, the pulsations become exaggerated and the network of pain nerves is stretched and pulled. Often during a one-sided attack a person can see and feel the arteries of the scalp standing out, especially on the painful side. The stretching effort on the expanded arteries provides only part of the pain. In addition there is produced locally in the tissues a certain chemical that increases sensitivity to pain.

You may have noticed that, in the midst of your own headache attack, such usually painless activities as pressing on the scalp or combing your hair becomes painful. Not only are tactile sensations exaggerated during migraine, but also bright lights, loud noises, and even pungent odors become particularly annoying. It is as if the nerves, not only in the tissues surrounding the painful artery but also in the central nervous system, are set to respond to most sensations in an exaggerated way.

Who Gets Migraine Headaches? Susceptibility to migraine reflects a number of contributory factors, the first of which is inborn (genetic). One of the authors of this chapter (Helen Goodell), in collaboration with a geneticist, carefully documented the family histories of 119 patients with migraine. From her findings, she concluded that susceptibility to migraine headache is indeed hereditary and is probably transmitted by a recessive gene with a 70 percent penetrance. To put it another way, when both parents have migraine, about 70 percent of the offspring also will experience migraine.

In most so-called hereditary disorders, the actual manifestation of the hereditary trait depends upon other factors, chiefly environmental. A vast number of factors may be related, such as a person's upbringing, the demands made upon that person by the people and circumstances that surround him, and his choice of activities and the satisfaction he derives from them. In short, the person's temperament, which is partly hereditary and partly shaped by environment, is basic to his susceptibility to migraine headache.

Portrait of a Migraineur. The migraineur is usually considered by others to be conscientious, reliable, hard working, well dressed and well mannered, and not in any sense a nervous person. Consequently, migraineurs are found frequently among those in positions of responsibility and trust. While migraineurs are not nervous in the usual sense they are likely to have, in common with so many of us, feelings of self-doubt, or even guilt and at times intense anger. The highly disciplined migraineur hides these feelings, often even from himself. To compensate he strives to be above criticism, to never appear in an unfavorable light, and to never be caught off guard. In setting high standards for himself and those about him he may at times seem frustrated and intolerant.

In all his endeavors the migraineur strives to perform in an exemplary fashion and hence he is likely to work harder and longer than his colleagues.

A day off from work is not necessarily a pleasant experience for him. Instead of enjoying peace and relaxation, he may feel guilty because he's wasting time, not getting anything done. He does not like to take part in spur-of-the-moment outings, only likes activities that are well planned in advance. He does not develop intimate relationships easily and finds it difficult to "let his hair down." Despite this lack of easy informality and spontaneity, migraineurs often make the most dependable, generous and loyal friends.

What Gives the Migraineur a Headache? It is important to realize that stress does not bring on migraine headaches in everyone, but only in those who are susceptible to migraine. Even in susceptible individuals, a crisis, when coped with successfully, can bring that rare feeling of achievement and satisfaction to the migraineur. However, the same crisis could be followed the next day by an excruciating headache if he felt that he had not handled the situation in the best possible way. Similarly, the death of a loved one might bring sorrow, but no trace of headache. However, should a feeling of guilt be associated with the death, as, for example, in the case of a daughter who felt she had not devoted enough time or care to her elderly mother, severe migraines might recur for a prolonged period of time.

Headaches are more likely to occur in association with a vague or even unconscious feeling of not "pulling your own weight." A woman may find it difficult to be a house guest and to let her hostess provide for her comfort; she will feel far more comfortable if she is allowed to help with the cooking, the cleaning, or some other productive activity. A migraineur who joins a club will wind up doing far more than his share of the work lest other members consider him a "goldbrick."

The timing of the headache depends on a variety of factors. It may appear that a headache is brought on by a trivial circumstance: a stuffy room; a hot, humid day; a loud siren; a dripping faucet. In reality, these trivial stimuli trigger a headache only if the person is "set" for one by such tension producing situations as long preparation for a test, or frantic overwork to meet a deadline.

In the setting of tension, when the patient is ready for a headache, the slightest disappointment, resentment, or frustration might set off a headache. During the long-dreaded meeting with prospective in-laws, a single cocktail might set off a headache in a person who normally has several drinks without feeling any effect. Alcohol is capable of dilating the blood vessels. When living at a level of stress and fatigue, the individual becomes increasingly vulnerable to painful stretching of his blood vessels. The pain may even begin during sleep, so that the patient awakens with a throbbing headache and an angry, frustrated, sick feeling.

Treatment of Migraine Headache. Treatment may proceed along these lines: First, the mechanism of bodily disturbances is carefully explained. Next, the patient is encouraged to recognize the connection between his headaches and the way he meets life's problems. The study of his own temperament and patterns of reaction may yield an insight into how he got that way, i.e., the beginnings of his attitudes and behavior. Then possible ways of modifying existing situations are discussed, as well as the need to change his attitudes and ways of dealing with problems.

Gunnar G. Sevelius, M.D.

Finally, he is given reassurance and moral support and is made to understand that his headaches are an outgrowth of the way he deals with his circumstances. Soon he learns to recognize the precipitating factors for each of his headaches, and is often able to avoid them by dealing differently with relevant people and events.

The simple pain relievers recommended for the occasional tension headache have little value for the treatment of the intense pain of a migraine headache. The most appropriate medicine, ergo-tamine, is not a pain reliever at all but a constrictor of blood vessels, therefore the drug blocks the pain mechanism rather than blocking pain sensation. It should be given very early in the headache to be fully effective. Ergotamine is most effective when given by injection but can be taken by mouth or as a suppository in combination with caffeine which enhances its absorption from the intestinal tract and also acts as a milder con stricter of arteries. Once a migraine attack has begun in full force it is better for the patient to "tough it out" rather than to load himself with useless painkillers or sedatives. They simply won't do the job and the subsequent hazards that may result especially from meperidine (Demerol), codeine, oxycodone (Percodan) and other narcotic preparations may simply perpetuate the headache and especially the nausea and vomiting. It is usually because of such misguided management that a severe migraine attack may last for several days. Such *status migrainous,* accompanied as it is by dehydration and physical and emotional exhaustion can be extremely debilitating. Admitted to the hospital, the patient is best treated with a proper balance of intravenous fluids, close attention, encouragement and time.

All sedative and narcotic drugs are to be avoided. To do so may take considerable fortitude and diplomacy on the part of the attending physician. In the end, however, the patient benefits and his recovery is speeded.

There have been efforts to prevent migraine attacks through the daily administration of methysergide (Sansert). The complications of long-term use, however, especially scarring in the lungs and elsewhere require that the patient be monitored very closely. Propranolol and certain other drugs that block impulses in the sympathetic nervous system have been effective in preventing attacks but their use also requires considerable supervision. The safest and most lasting prevention comes from the patient learning to head off an attack through enhanced knowledge of himself gained with the help of a perceptive and committed physician. Most headache sufferers come to the doctor with no inkling of a disordered life adjustment. The physician, therefore, must be patient and often subtle as he helps his patient learn about himself as a unique individual functioning in a social setting with his own special job to be done. The values and aspirations peculiar to him must be considered as well as the requirements of his job.

From a vast number of experiences, humans have been shown, but have not altogether learned, that health and well-being depend not only on a capacity to adapt to the tangible environment, but also to prevailing attitudes and values in society and to a person's own goals and aspirations.

OTHER REASONS FOR PAIN
IN BLOOD VESSELS

TUMORS. Brain tumors cause pain mainly because they take up space in a closed box (the skull), displacing and stretching pain sensitive structures, especially the blood vessels that anchor the brain at its base and on its upper surface. Pressure on and displacement of portions of the brain itself by the tumor usually causes signs and symptoms such as dizziness, deafness, weakness of an area or a leg or balancing difficulty. These can be picked up by an examining physician.

FEVER. Headaches that occur with most fevers are due to stretching of the walls of the arteries within the head brought on by increased blood flow in most of the body. When a fever-producing infection is located within the head, the headache is, of course, more severe. Such infections may occur in the meninges, the envelope of the brain through which the blood vessels travel, or there may be an abscess in the substance of the brain which displaces pain sensitive structures and produces pain jut as tumors do. This is a medical emergency requiring immediate medical treatment.

ALCOHOL. The familiar "hangover" headache comes from a combination of consequences of over indulgence. First of all, alcohol expands blood vessels and may thus contribute to headache in people susceptible to migraine and other vascular headaches. Add to this the stress of a party, fatigue and sometimes concern or guilt about one's behavior. The morning headaches of severe alcoholics are further contributed to by dehydration and general disruption of the body's chemical equilibrium.

HIGH BLOOD PRESSURE. Blood vessel, or vascular headaches are common among those with high blood pressure. It is usually not the pressure within the blood vessel that causes headache but instead a painful expansion of arteries very similar to that which characterize migraine (previously discussed). While a very sudden rise in blood pressure is capable of providing pain, as for example, after a rapid injection of adrenaline, the chronic headache of the patient with hypertension (high blood pressure) cannot be attributed to the prevailing blood pressure level. In fact, the headache has been shown to be independent of fluctuations in blood pressure. On the other hand, hypertensive patients, like those with migraine often are susceptible to vascular headache. Indeed, their headaches may have been recurrent and troublesome long before their blood pressure rose to hypertensive levels. The treatment of patients with headache associated with hypertension has to be directed to the control of the high blood pressure but is also similar to that of other headache sufferers. Especially important is learning to relax, learning about oneself, and learning to deal more smoothly with problems and conflicts of day-to-day life. (See Part I, High Blood Pressure).

SUMMARY

Most people suffer from headaches. For the most part, this is nothing more than an occasional nuisance. Pain can be controlled by using aspirin, acetaminophen, ibuprofen, Aleve, or one of several prescription medications. A primary concern is the chronic, recurrent, or persistent painful headache that may require medical attention.

A variety of factors—hereditary, mechanical, situational and emotional enter into the mechanisms that cause headaches. The commonest mechanisms involve tightness of muscles in the neck, scalp and face and stretching or displacement of the major arteries outside or inside the skull.

Prevention and treatment depends upon the specific cause of the headache. When emotional stress is the main cause, stress reduction techniques may alleviate the problem and sometimes the underlying problem can be resolved through effective communi-cation with loved ones, or through professional counseling. When using medicines, caution should be exercised with regard to drugs that are potentially addictive. Ask your physician about the drugs that you take routinely for headache pain.

Keep in mind that the drugs to reduce headache pain (including aspirin) only treat the symptom. For occasional headaches this is fine but for a person who suffers recurring headaches, the only effective relief is gained by treating the cause of the problem. Rather than trying to self-diagnose and self-medicate, it is advisable to consult your family doctor. If the incidents continue to occur, ask your physician to recommend a clinic that specializes in headache pain.

FAMILY SOCIAL SUPPORT

How Positive Forces Can Make You

Healthier and Happier

John G. Bruhn, Ph. D.

LIFE'S MIRROR

There are loyal hearts, there are spirits brave,
There are souls that are pure and true;
Then give to the world the best you have,
And the best will come back to you.

Give love, and love to your life will flow,
A strength in your utmost need;
Have faith, and a score of hearts will show.
Their faith in your word and deed.

Give truth, and your gift will be paid in kind,
And honor will honor meet;
And a smile that is sweet will surely find
A smile that is just as sweet.

Give sorrow and pity to those who mourn;
You will gather in flowers again
The scattered seeds of your thought outborne,
Though the sowing seemed but vain.

For life is the mirror of king and slave
'Tis just what we are and do;
Then give to the world the best you have,
And the best will come back to you.

MADELINE BRIDGES

INTRODUCTION

Newspaper and magazine features, television specials, movies, and, for many, first hand experiences have made us aware of major changes in American family life. Marriage rates have dropped and divorce rates have increased. Fertility levels have declined, illegitimacy rates have climbed, and men and women have sought to live alone in increasing numbers. Many have concluded that the traditional American family as we once knew it, is dead.

Americans, nostalgically, have always held onto the ideal of the traditional family—how family life ought to be. That ideal included: a nice suburban home, a breadwinner husband and a homemaker wife, two children, two cars, and the latest appliances. However, as our society has changed, the needs of individuals have changed, and, in turn, the ideal of the family has become more unrealistic.

Increasingly there will be a great diversity in the lifestyles of families and individuals. Households will be smaller; they will change more often. There will be more two-worker households and more households in which men and women live alone. These new kinds of households will change the nature of cities, create new kinds of markets for different consumer goods and leisure activities, and place new demands on public programs. They will create new challenges for the economy, the community, and the government.

While the nature of the family has changed, some of its traditional functions and responsibilities have not changed. One of these functions is to provide a sense of security and personal well-being, or social support for family members. The family has traditionally been a place to learn how to successfully cope with the world outside the family and a place to return to for understanding and encouragement when crises occur. Family members were available to help each other. While family social support takes different forms for different families, the need for social support exists in some degree in all families, whatever their composition.

CHANGES IN FAMILY LIFE

The following statistics chronicle the drastic changes in the structure of family life:

- Nearly half of all marriages end in divorce.
- An estimated 40 percent of the children born in this decade will spend at least part of their youth in homes with only one parent.
- Households headed by women have doubled in the last generation and increased by a third in the last ten years.
- A third of the women with children under age three work outside the home.
- The percentage of people aged 20-34 who have never married has increased by 10 to 20 percent in the last 16 years.
- The number of unmarried couples living together has more than doubled since 1960.

As social beings we are givers and takers of social support. Some health professionals feel that social support is necessary in helping people to stay well and affects their recovery when they are sick. As our society changes, social support becomes even more important as an aid in coping with life events. This text will examine the following questions regarding social support:

What is social support? What is family social support? What are the benefits of social support? What are the sources of social support? What can you do to make social support available and beneficial to you?

SOCIAL SUPPORT

Social support is behavior that gives us nurturance and provides reinforcement for our efforts to cope with life on a daily basis. Social support provides us with the courage to take risks, to take on new challenges, and to successfully complete difficult tasks. Social support is a cushion or buffer in times of stress or crisis. Each of us is capable of giving support to others as well as of receiving it. We all have different needs for social support at different times in our lives. Sometimes it is difficult to ask for support when we feel we need it and sometimes we are offered support when we feel we don't need it. The need for social support is a personal matter. What is important is that we don't take social support for granted. We need to develop new sources of support as well as nurture old ones. Social support should be a part of our daily life and not something we need to think about only when we have problems.

FAMILY SOCIAL SUPPORT

The family is a source of social support we usually count on. We expect parents, brothers, sisters, and relatives to be on our side and to be available to give us support when we need it. Sometimes the family is not supportive and we look to others for help. As the family changes, the ability of family members to be supportive of each other may change. Indeed, we may feel closer to one particular family member than to others. That is the person we look to for advice and in whom we confide, and that is the person who gives us encouraging words to keep trying, whatever our goals may be.

Family social support helps us to grow as persons. We learn how important it is to be helpful and hopeful. We learn that social support can help us to live healthier and happier lives when we are able both to give and receive social support.

THE BENEFITS OF SOCIAL SUPPORT

The major benefits of social support could be called the three H's—Health, Happiness, and Hope.

Health. Some researchers have found that under conditions of high life change or chronic exposure to stress, social support buffers individuals from potential adverse effects and helps them to cope and adapt, reducing the likelihood of illness. One study found that men who experienced high levels of anxiety and who perceived their wives as unloving and unsupportive were more likely to develop chest pain than men who experienced anxiety, but reported that their wives were loving and supportive. In still another study, it was reported that mothers who had supportive family members had fewer complications during labor and delivery than did women who had little or no social support. It is not always true that good health will result if a person has strong social support or that poor health will result if a person has little or no social support. When we speak of health, however, we include psychological and spiritual as well as physical health. Social support provides encouragement and heightens our morale, which, in turn, motivates us to stay well or to get well when we are sick.

Happiness. Social support can have an effect on our total well-being or happiness. We all have a need to belong and to be loved. Some psychologists suggest that our need to be loved can predominate even over our physiological needs.

Our earliest experiences with love and intimacy are usually with our parents or siblings. When these relationships are successful, that success enriches life and provides a source of strength and support. As we grow, the ability to achieve intimacy with people outside the family becomes an intensely felt need, and is necessary for self-esteem, since the ability to have friends, to love, and to be loved is highly valued.

In a close relationship, we can feel accepted. Most people experience at least one such close relationship during elementary and high school. Following high school graduation, it is common for friends to be physically separated as they go off to different jobs or colleges. Individuals then need to develop new intimate relationships. This pattern may be repeated many times throughout life. While not all relationships are intimate, all relationships are part of the search for some kind of love or belongingness.

All of us need to feel needed. The way we see ourselves shapes other people's reactions to us. At the same time, their reactions affect the way we regard ourselves. Our self-image is part of a continuous cycle, which either confirms our favorable feelings about ourselves or reinforces negative feelings. We need social support to reinforce our good feelings and to help us put our negative feelings in proper perspective.

Not all of our physiological and psychological needs can be satisfied at any given time. There is always a gap of dissatisfaction; at times, the gap becomes wide. This may happen when we feel unloved, when we feel we have failed at a task, let someone down, not lived up to our expectations, or when we feel lonely, isolated, and unsupported. We all have unique ways of coping with our periods of dissatisfaction. We may eat, drink, smoke, sleep, work, dream, or use more healthy means of coping such as talking things out, thinking things through, problem solving, and seeking the advice of friends. A life without problems or stress is probably not worth living and in any event is impossible. What makes the difference to well-being is not merely the nature of the problem, but the way we experience it and react to it.

We often tend not to reach or experience our full potential in life. Social support from others can help us continue to experience our full potential and maintain a feeling of fulfillment in life. To achieve happiness, we need others and others need us. How happy are you? Are your needs being met? Are you helping others to meet their needs?

Hope. Our attitude toward life can affect our health. Indeed, our attitude tells a lot about how we cope with daily life and the unexpected problems we all encounter. The attitudes of hope and hopelessness are ways of coping. They reflect our estimate of the probability of achieving certain goals. A hopeless person believes that plans of action are no longer effective in reaching goals and may, as a consequence, feel helpless. When a person feels that whatever he does is futile and that there is no hope, illness and even death may follow. To give up hope is to give up zest for living. To give up hope is to abandon plans for the future.

A hopeful attitude, on the other hand, indicates that we want to look forward to the future, whatever it may bring. A hopeful person enjoys life despite its problems. A hopeful person looks at problems as challenges to be mastered. A hopeful person believes in himself and others. Although we know little about how hope is given or lost, there is evidence that hope, like faith and a purpose in life, is therapeutic.

Attitude affects our physical and psychological health. Some researchers believe that a depressed or hopeless attitude can suppress our immune system so that we become more susceptible to infections and malignant diseases. An attitude of hopelessness among those who are sick may inhibit their recovery—they may make less effort to help themselves get well because they may feel they have little to look forward to. We all need hope to stay well.

Through hope we retain communication with relatives, friends, jobs, and organizations in which we invest ourselves. It is through these social connections that we receive and give social support. Social support is an expression of hope. There is evidence that supportive interactions among people are protective against the consequences of stress. Knowing that others can share your problems and successes is comforting and, indeed, that knowledge alone can often provide the strength we need to survive tough times.

We all need to have our hope replenished periodically. Some people find such replenishment through religious belief and activities. Others are replenished through volunteer and community work. Still others seek replenishment through solitude. There are many different ways to restore hope. The ways we choose to do this depend on our personal needs.

Some practical suggestions are offered to help you remain hopeful and healthy:

1. Try not to let stressful problems get the best of you. Learn new ways to control stress. (See Part I, Stress Management), to relax, and to maintain a positive attitude in solving problems.
2. Focus on the positive rather than the negative aspects of your life; find satisfaction in your accomplishments.
3. Remain involved with people so that you are an active part of a social network that can become a source of support.
4. Take time for yourself and time to replenish your sources of hope.
5. Establish some long-term goals that require you to plan for and look forward to the future.

SOURCES OF SOCIAL SUPPORT

Every human has the need for companionship and for the reassurance and emotional security, which comes from belonging to a social unit whose members share the same ideas and patterns of behavior. It is possible for some people to live by themselves—for a time. St. Francis of Assisi was able to live in solitary contemplation in the Italian countryside. Most people find that the experience of living in a community is an essential condition of survival. No one knows why a healthy person will deteriorate if deprived of contact with his fellows. One source of support is our community—our neighbors and the familiar surroundings of our neighborhood.

Religious beliefs are another source of social support. There is a need for stability, security, and hope, which spiritual belief helps to satisfy. Religious rituals may serve to reinforce our belief and remind us that there is a sense of purpose to our existence. This belief may be very comforting when we sometimes feel helpless and question the purpose of our existence. Our fellows who share our beliefs may be further evidence that we are not alone in our problems.

Organizations, clubs, self-help groups, and a variety of interest groups assemble individuals with common interests, goals, and talents to reinforce the importance of the individual to the group and the power of the group to bring about positive change. The group can be an effective way to accomplish things the individual, alone, cannot and, in this way, may provide individuals with a feeling of accom-plishment and good will. Many organizations have a history that extends beyond the lifetime of any individual member and, therefore, individual members have a sense of transmitting a legacy.

Work provides a source of social support for many individuals. Work is important in our society. We, therefore, receive a lot of positive reinforcement when we work. Work consumes most of the time; for a lot of people work provides identity and pride. Work colleagues can be very supportive and become close friends.

The family is still a key source of social support. The family adapted to our technological age by taking advantage of the freedom of choice that technology offers. There is less emphasis on formal structure dictating who is to do what to whom and for whom. The distinctions between male and female roles have blurred. People visit their relatives on the basis of which ones they get along with best, not on the basis of ties of genealogy.

These changes have not weakened the family. It is still the "place where, when you go there, they take you in."

NEED FOR SOCIAL SUPPORT AT VARIOUS LIFE STAGES

Infancy. The parental bond and bonds between members of the family provide the first experiences with social support. A parent-infant interaction pattern may be established as early as a few days after birth. Bonding implies togetherness and interdependence, not only in withstanding threatening forces outside the bonded unit, but also in sharing personal values and behavioral expectations. Bonds provide the sense of security an individual needs to grow and to be able to risk new experiences. When the sense of bondedness is secure, each family member feels the security he needs to face challenges, and the support he needs if he fails. Bonds change over time. Family bonds must change to allow individuals to grow into mature adults. The nature and quality of bonds change as the needs of individuals change.

The nature of individuals' early experiences with bonding helps to shape their perceptions and expectations of social support and the degree to which support becomes a part of their coping repertoire. People who are in trouble may be those who believe that they have no one to call upon for help, who cannot ask for help or accept it when they need to, or who lack the skill or foresight to cultivate supportive relationships. Social support, however, is not only an antidote for crisis, but a source of nurturance during relatively tranquil times. Individuals who recognize an ongoing need for social support are usually effective in becoming an integrated part of social networks which provide continuous or "maintenance levels" of support. These networks change as people age or change their environments. Therefore, there is a life-long challenge to continuously develop new sources of social support. The experiences with bonding in infancy influence an individual's later ability to develop new sources of support.

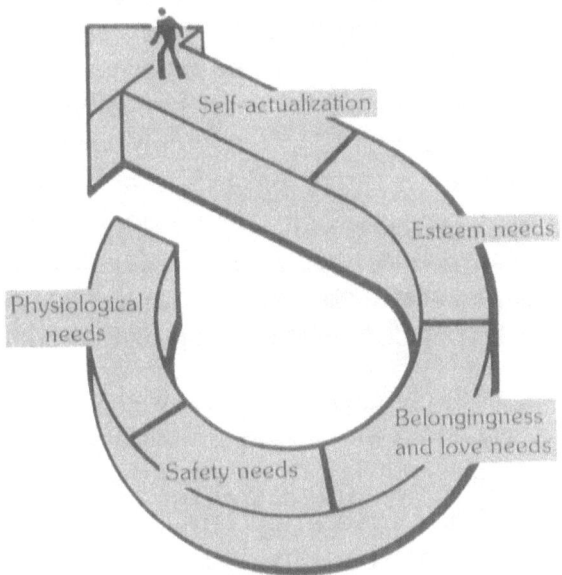

Erik Erikson, the father of modern psychology, proposed that, in infancy, the most crucial sense to be formed is a sense of trust, a feeling of confidence that caregivers can be relied upon to provide adequate care. Erikson's sense of trust does not explicitly deal with bonding or attachment; however, it is implicit in his theory that an attachment does form between the infant and the caregiver as trust develops. Erikson suggested that when a primary caregiver meets an infant's needs with sameness and continuity, the infant learns to rely, not only on the external provider, but also on himself.

The kind of adults that infants become is certainly influenced by caregivers and by the care received, but behaviors of caregivers do not create the whole personality of adults. Social development is multifaceted, with both infants and adults affecting the outcomes. Each infant has his or her unique characteristics for seeking or avoiding stimuli, and for interpreting and adapting to experiences.

While social development follows a pattern, all children do not learn social skills in the same way. There are cultural variations in social development and in learning and experiencing social support. Child-rearing practices are very responsive to environmental conditions. In life-threatening environments, for example, safety is enhanced by a greater physical proximity between mother and child. In societies where food and subsistence items are scarce, parents teach behaviors that would ensure later physical self-maintenance. While families from different cultures and socioeconomic levels have different priorities and values, social support appears to be an aspect of human behavior that is common to people in all cultures.

Early Childhood. The characteristic ways of relating to people become pronounced in early childhood. With the development of autonomy and initiative, children begin to detach themselves from their parents. They explore new territory, learn new games, and form new relationships with peers. Friends become as important as parents.

The warmth that parents show exerts a strong influence on whether their children will emulate them. The influence of the father seems especially important in sex typing, since fathers usually respond differently to sons and daughters, while mothers treat their children more similarly.

"Goldie is not a good pet. She is hard to hug."

How parents deal with children's fears, actual and imagined, harbors important messages about social support for the child. The best ways to help children overcome fears involve activity by the children, themselves. Children are most successful when they find their own practical methods to deal with what they fear and when they are gradually helped to experience frightening situations. Modeling, or showing fearlessness in others, is helpful.

Different parenting styles (authoritarian, permissive, and harmonious) encourage different personality traits in children and result in different experiences with social support.

Contributions of the Family to the Development of Children

- Feelings of security from being a member of a stable group.
- People children can rely on to meet their needs—physical and psychological.
- Sources of affection and acceptance, regardless of what they do.
- Models of approved patterns of behavior for learning to be social.
- Guidance in the development of socially approved patterns of behavior.
- People they can turn to for help in solving the problems every child faces in adjustment to life.
- Guidance and help in learning skills—motor verbal, and social—needed for adjustment.
- Stimulation of their abilities to achieve success in school and in social life.
- Aid in setting aspirations suited to their interests and abilities.
- Sources of companionship until old enough to find companions outside the home or when outside companionship is unavailable.

Late Childhood. Peer groups often impose their own dominance on the emerging individual. Peer groups help children form attitudes and values; they provide a forum for sifting through parental values and deciding which to keep and which to discard. Children learn how and when to adjust their desires to others, when to yield, and when to stand firm. Peer groups are support groups when members conform to group standards.

One of the most important aspects of development is a favorable self-concept. Self-concept is a reflection of an individual's degree of confidence in coping with obstacles and in problem solving.

Although a child spends a great deal of time with peers, the family is still an important influence. Children grow up in a variety of family situations. An atmosphere of love, support, and respect for family members provides an important ingredient for later healthy development.

Early Adolescence and Adolescence. One of the most important tasks of adolescence is the search for identity. The adolescent seeks an image he does not know in a world he rarely understands, with a body that he is just discovering. He desires to assert himself at the same time he fears the loss of the security and reassurance of his family.

The stage of adolescence is one of change and individual variation. It is the stage that bridges childhood and adulthood. Psychologically, adoles-cence involves the struggle to be independent from one's parents, develop a system of values, and form mature relationships of friendship and love. This stage involves testing and developing new types of social support as well as learning to cope in situations with and without "natural" or expected sources of support.

Early Adulthood. During this developmental period, individuals choose their life paths and begin to walk independently along them. Young adults choose their careers, decide on family lifestyles, establish networks of friends, engage in leisure activities, and begin to invest time in civic and community activities. Individuals begin to develop and expand their social support networks. This developmental period is relatively free from the crises of adolescence; young adults are somewhat secure in their identity and have ability to cope independently with problems.

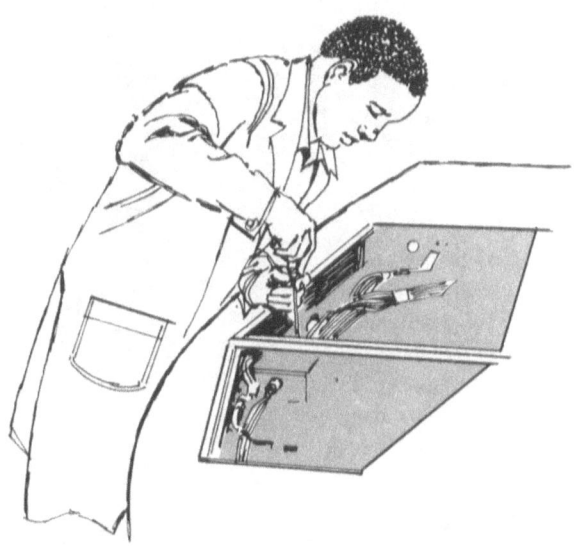

Middle Adulthood. The main focus in this developmental period is on reevaluating oneself and one's life. Personality continues to change as a result of the experiences, relationships, and self-evaluation that occur during this period. In general, individuals experience a sense of competence and power and enjoy the fruits of their years of experience. Health and other problems among friends, relatives, and family members begin to emerge, calling upon individuals to mobilize and utilize sources of social support. This stage of life is generally positive, despite the common assumption that mid-life involves the trauma associated with nostalgia for youth, fears of aging, and the self-concept of a middle-aged person.

Maturity. As in every other stage of the life cycle, no arbitrary dividing line determines when middle age ends and old age begins. The diversity present throughout life is still present and, in fact, appears to be more pronounced in old age than in earlier years. We have labeled the final developmental period "maturity", to avoid the negative stereotypes that are elicited when the terms, "elderly", "senior citizens", etc., are used. Maturity has many positive attributes and, indeed, mature individuals become sources of social support, not only to peers, but to younger people. Individuals who have experienced life's problems and successes are able to provide perspective and guidance about what has worked effectively for them. Mature adults may need to reorganize their daily lives to meet the requirements of retirement, changes in their health and vitality, and, perhaps, the death of a spouse or family member. This final stage is a normal period of the life span with its own special characteristics and its own developmental tasks.

How Supportive is Your Support System?

We need to take a periodic inventory to identify our available sources of social support. We need to reaffirm their availability should we need them. Sometimes our sources of support fall short of our expectations or just don't come through when we need them. If this is so, we need to either improve our sources of support or develop new ones.

Sources of support also need nourishment. We cannot expect to use sources of support without acknowledging their importance and replenishing them. Is your support system reciprocal? Are you putting something back into the system to be supportive to others?

What You Can Do to Make Social Support Available and Beneficial

While we all have the need for social support it is sometimes difficult for individuals to ask for support in a culture that emphasizes self-sufficiency and independence. Sometimes a request for love, attention, empathy, or a sympathetic ear is interpreted as a sign of weakness.

There are three steps that can help support become more available to you:

The first step is to reach out—extend yourself to others so that you can learn about each others' needs. A person who does not reach out to others cannot know what support is available, or may be needed.

A second step is to cultivate the ability to accept support when it is offered. Sometimes it is easier to decline the offer of support than to admit that we need it. We need to accept our humanness and the fact that we sometimes need assistance from others. We also need to realize that by accepting occasional help from others, we, in turn, help them to develop good feelings about themselves and also about ourselves.

A third step is to cultivate the ability to reciprocate in giving support. Some individuals find it easier to give support than to receive it, while others, seemingly, accept support without replenishing the supplier. More sources of support will become available to us if we reciprocate by giving support when others are in need of it. We need to develop a sensitivity to other people's need for support so that we will know when it is appropriate to offer support, regardless of whether it has been requested.

Social support is only beneficial if it assists us in our adaptation to life; it should not create dependency, stifle creativity, or encourage helplessness. Social support is beneficial to most people when it facilitates problem-solving, strengthens motivation, and restores equilibrium. Some types of social support may be considered beneficial by some persons and not by others. Social support is, perhaps, most effective when giving and receiving it become a natural part of everyday life.

SUMMARY

The family is a primary source of social support. The nature of the supportive mechanisms will vary from family to family. Social support gives us nurturance and helps us cope with life's problems. The primary benefits include health, happiness, and hope. The establishment of nurturing relationships helps to both reduce the intensity of a crisis as well as to prevent crisis from occurring. Social networks are helpful in facilitating problem solving, strengthening motivation, and restoring equilibrium.

Practical suggestions for reducing conflict are:

1. Keep problems in perspective—don't catastrophize.
2. Learn ways to relax in order to dissipate emotions.
3. Maintain a positive attitude and an "I can" spirit.
4. Find satisfaction in your accomplishments.
5. Develop a social network—don't let yourself become isolated.
6. Make time to enjoy life.
7. Develop a life-plan for attaining goals.
8. Cultivate the ability to accept and to give social support.

There are many resources available to individuals who want to develop social networks. Often, the workplace provides an employee recreation program and/or a wellness program. Clubs, teams and professional associations at the workplace also offer opportunity for growth, stimulation, and social support.

DRUG BASICS

Wes Alles, Ph.D.

Foreword by Edward N. Brandt, Jr., M.D., Ph.D.

*One of the first duties of the physician
is to educate the masses
not to take medicine or drugs.*

Idem

FOREWORD

Information and Communication. Two important words for most aspects of life, but they are vital when drugs or medications are concerned. Drugs sold legally in the United States are as safe as people can make them; *but only if they are used properly.* Hence, information is essential for the user, and communication with physicians and pharmacists can lead to that information and its attendant understanding.

This text is another method of communication. It contains useful, perhaps vital, information for you. Application of this information will lead to the most effective use of drugs and, therefore, to the greatest benefit to you.

One of the more important lessons to be learned is that medications are not always useful or helpful. For example, laxatives are rarely needed and their use can become habitual with no health benefit. The common cold requires time for resolution—most cold medicines may reduce your symptoms but they do not stop the disease.

This text is well written and full of good advice. Use of its contents will yield benefits to you and your family.

Good Health.

Edward N. Brandt, Jr., M.D., Ph.D.

DRUG BASICS

We hear a lot about drugs. Our newspapers, radios, and televisions are filled with information about drugs. Day-to-day conversation with friends and neighbors occasionally focus on drug use. The availability and use of these products in America raises many serious issues, particularly in regard to the illicit (illegal) drugs that capture the attention of the media. But there are many important issues related to legal drugs—drugs that most of us use routinely without giving them a second thought. This text deals with prescription medicines, over-the-counter drugs, and caffeine. It would be appropriate to discuss nicotine and alcohol in the context of this text, but they are covered in other chapters of this series.

Drugs are chemicals, other than food and water, that create actions and reactions within the body. Their use changes our biochemistry. We consume drugs because they do something for us and we select a particular drug because of its unique ability to create an action that we want. Drugs are capable of curing disease, relieving symptoms, altering our mood, pepping us up or calming us down, making us feel better than we did. Among the many beneficial effects, drugs can lower blood pressure, fight infection, regulate our hormones, relieve pain or discomfort, eliminate rashes, and destroy cancer cells. But anything that has the potential to do so much good also has the potential to create an action or reaction that we don't like—a consequence which is harmful to our mood, to our responsibilities, or to our body.

Sometimes drugs are used inappropriately. A person may select the wrong drug for a particular need. Misuse also occurs when the correct drug is selected but the person takes the wrong dosage (too little or too much) or follows the wrong schedule (too often or not often enough). Habitual use of drugs, without periodic evaluation of their effectiveness, also holds the potential for misuse as shown in the following illustration. Certainly, anytime the body's biochemistry is changed needlessly, or when the change is so severe that the body has a difficult time adjusting, drugs are being used inappropriately. Whenever we ingest a substance that can alter our internal environment, we have the responsibility to be properly informed and to carefully consider the pros and cons. Only in this way can we maximize the benefit and minimize the risk.

Sometimes the result of taking a drug is obvious, as when we take aspirin and our headache disappears, or when we take an antibiotic and our infection is cured. But oftentimes the reactions are not so obvious as when aspirin thins our blood and makes clotting difficult, or when antibiotics raise our sensitivity to sunlight making us more susceptible to sunburn. In addition to their intended effect, many of the drugs we take can produce body changes that we don't know about and which we might not enjoy. For instance, some of the side effects of drugs can make us sleepy, irritable, constipated, raise our blood pressure, or make us uninterested in sex. We are fortunate to have drugs so widely available, but the more we know about them, the more likely it is that we will be able to enjoy their full benefit.

The Best Healer is Still Mother Nature

GLOSSARY

In order to help you understand some of the concepts presented in this text, the following glossary is provided. Take a minute to review the words and definitions.

Acetaminophen—This is a generic name for over-the-counter drugs that relieve pain and reduce fever. They may be used instead of aspirin. Examples are Tylenol and Datril.

Addiction—syn. Physical Dependence—The body needs the drug in order to avoid withdrawal symptoms. Examples include heroin, barbiturates, and some amphetamines, including caffeine.

Amphetamines—Drugs that speed up (stimulate) the central nervous system.

Analgesic—Pain relieving drugs such as aspirin, acetaminophen, ibuprofen, Demerol, and morphine.

Anaphylactic Reaction—A body response when a person is hypersensitive to a substance that is eaten, injected, absorbed, or smelled. Typical reactions include respiratory distress, hives, and itching.

Antianxiety Drug—Prescription medicines that counteract depression; e.g., Valium and Librium.

Antitussant—A drug that helps to relieve coughs. Normally they contain an expectorant to loosen the mucus and make the cough productive, and a cough suppressant to dull the cough reflex.

Barbiturates—Non-narcotic sedative drugs that slow down the central nervous system. Some are useful as anti-convulsants. Barbiturates are physically addicting.

Brand Name Drugs—These are drugs sold under registered trademark name owned by a particular company. Over-the-counter drugs have brand names for acetaminophen such as Tylenol and Datril. Prescription drugs have brand names such as Miltown and Equanil instead of the generic name meprobromate.

Contraindication—Certain physical or emotional conditions prohibit the use of some drugs. For instance, pregnancy is a contraindication for many drugs because the drug might affect the fetus. Diabetes, hypertension, arthritis, thyroid disease, and kidney disease are only a few of the conditions for which certain drugs should be avoided.

Downers—Depressant drugs that slow down the central nervous system such as tranquilizers, alcohol, and barbiturates.

Drug Dependence—A state of physical or psychological dependence that creates a continuing need for use of the drug.

Habituation—Compulsive use of drugs. The products are used as a habit to relieve symptoms; e.g., nasal sprays or eyewashes. People who habitually use a drug become psychologically dependent upon its effect.

Libido—This term refers to a person's sex drive. Some drugs affect libido. Most of these drugs lower it. Examples include alcohol, amphetamines, reserpine and tranquilizers. With the loss of sexual appetite, it is important to know if the drug is responsible.

Over-the-Counter (OTC)—These are drugs that are sold over-the-counter without a prescription at pharmacies or supermarkets. Examples include antacids, cold remedies, and sleep aids. These drugs are often called patent medicines. Over-the-counter drugs are good for the relief of symptoms only. Generally, they are not capable of curing a condition.

Although they are safe when taken as directed, they may not be as effective as advertisers would lead you to believe.

Photosensitivity—Some drugs increase the effect of ultraviolet rays on the skin, thereby producing sunburn or sun poisoning. Two commonly taken drugs of this type are tetracycline and oral contraceptives.

Physician's Desk Reference (PDR)—This annual publication describes drug action, contraindications, warnings, side effects, and other information for safe use. Most physician offices and libraries have them. Consumers should be encouraged to learn about their medication since it is their body that is being affected. The PDR is one source of information.

Drug Interaction—When more than one drug or medicine is taken, they can interact to produce a harmful, strange, or unusual result. For instance, aspirin taken at the same time as an anticoagulant produces such thin blood that bleeding may occur spontaneously. Over-the-counter drugs, prescription medicines, alcohol, and food are capable of producing an unwanted drug interaction.

Euphoria—An exaggerated sense of well-being.

Functional Dependence—Some drugs that are used to relieve symptoms take over normal body functions, and therefore, require that the drug be continued in order to maintain that function. For instance, prolonged use of laxatives may create the need for external stimulation in order to avoid constipation.

Generic Drugs—All drugs have an official name assigned to them. For example, ibuprofen is a generic name that can be used by any manufacturer. But only one company can use the brand name Motrin for the prescription drug, or Nuprin for the less potent over-the-counter drug. Generic drugs cost less than their brand name equivalent, even though they are exactly the same product chemically. Whenever you have a prescription filled ask your druggist if you can have the generic version.

You will save money and still get the benefit of the prescribed drug. This is particularly advantageous if you have a chronic condition that requires prolonged medication. Many companies have arrangements with mail order firms which allow for even greater savings. Check with your company representative.

Physical Dependence—see Addiction.

Potentiating Effect—syn. Synergistic effect—Sometimes the combined effect of two or more drugs will produce an effect far greater than either drug by itself. This can be extremely dangerous because the total effect may make it difficult for the body to adjust. Examples include alcohol and tranquilizers; or amphetamines and coffee.

Psychoactive Drug—Any drug that produces altered perceptions, feelings, moods or sensory experience.

Side Effects—These are known reactions to a drug that are not part of the intended therapeutic action. Most side effects are undesirable such as drowsiness, nausea, blurred vision, etc. The benefit of the drug must be weighted against the unwanted side effects.

Synergistic Effect—see Potentiating Effect.

Therapeutic Dose—This is the amount of a drug that will produce the desired effect. Less than this amount will be ineffective and a greater dose will not be more effective. This is one reason to follow the directions exactly as indicated.

Tolerance—This is when an ever-increasing quantity of the drug is needed to derive the desired effect. Drugs that produce tolerance are dangerous because at some point the higher dose will cause harm to the body.

Toxicity—This word refers to poisoning effect. Many drugs are safe when used as directed but become toxic with high doses or prolonged use.

Withdrawal Symptoms—Some drugs can produce withdrawal symptoms, e.g, nicotine, caffeine, and alcohol. When the person doesn't receive a sufficient dose the body reacts with symptoms that include headache, cramps, perspiration, insomnia, diarrhea, irritability, and hallucinations.

PRESCRIPTION DRUGS RX

Pharmaceutical products are researched, developed, tested, and marketed at great expense. After thorough testing and documentation the drugs must be approved by the Food and Drug Administration (FDA). The company that develops the drug is given the exclusive right to sell that product for 17 years. This helps to retrieve the costs of research and development. A committee will assign the drug an official name and the original company will develop a brand name. During the 17-year period, the company will market the drug under its brand name so that physicians and consumers become familiar with it. After this period of time other licensed companies can sell the drug under the official name or under its own brand name. The official name is also known as the generic name. For instance, penicillin, cortisone, and prednisone are generic names.

**Particularly Advantageous if You Have a
Chronic Condition that Requires Prolonged Medication**

Physicians can prescribe drugs using either the generic or brand name. For a variety of reasons it is usually less expensive for the consumer when the generic name is used. In this case the pharmacist may use any of the brand names that are available. In some cases there is a question as to whether drugs that are chemically alike actually perform equally well inside the body. This issue is known as bioavailability. In the majority of cases bioavailability is the same and generic drugs can save a substantial amount of money. But in some cases your physician may prefer to prescribe a brand name because of previous results using that drug. When you receive. a prescription, ask your doctor about this issue.

Prescription medicines are powerful chemicals that can dramatically alter a person's biochemistry. That is why a prescription is necessary in order to obtain the drug. The physician's directions should be followed exactly in order to derive maximum benefit. For instance, the dose and frequency are important to therapeutic effect. Food in the stomach can alter absorption. Some drugs can be taken with food while others need to be taken on an empty stomach. Most drugs should be taken with water since the stomach pH affects the release of medicine. For instance, tetracycline should not be taken with dairy products because the drug may pass through the body without being broken down. Also, drugs can interfere with food so that nutrients contained in the food are not absorbed into the bloodstream for metabolism.

An important issue is drug interaction. Some drugs in combination produce a potentiating effect (synergistic), while in other cases one drug may neutralize the effect of another. In either case, the therapeutic dose is altered and the desirable effect will not be achieved. This interaction can occur when both drugs are prescription, when one or both drugs are over-the-counter preparations, or when certain foods or alcohol are consumed with either prescription or over-the-counter medicines. Doctors can help you prevent an unwanted drug interaction. Pharmacists, too, are excellent sources of information, especially if you are taking over-the-counter drugs that have not been prescribed by your doctor.

A particularly dangerous drug interaction occurs with medicines that contain monoamine oxidase (MAO) inhibitors. Monoamine oxidase is present in the body. Tyramine is present in a number of foods and beverages. The effect of tyramine is to raise blood pressure to a dangerously high level. Normally, MAO will counteract the tyramine and blood pressure remains normal. But when a person consumes a drug with an MAO inhibitor, the tyramine can cause serious problems with high blood pressure. MAO inhibiting drugs are marked to warn the consumer. It is your responsibility to determine which foods should not be eaten.

People with chronic disease and the elderly are especially in need of drug information. Chronic disease often requires continuous medication and adjustment by the body to the chemical changes. With multiple health problems, people may need multiple medications. The possibility of unwanted drug interaction is high so a person should always check with his/her physician—even when choosing over-the-counter drugs. Additionally, the person may want to develop a system for taking the proper pill at the correct time. One good system is to use an egg carton that contains 12 egg wells. Times of the day can be written on the inside top of the container and pills then can be dropped into the appropriate well. This enables the individual to determine whether a dose was missed anytime during the day.

Storage of prescription drugs presents another issue. Pills should always be stored out of the reach of children. The bedroom is not the best storage site because there might be a tendency to awaken in the middle of the night and reach for a pill in the dark. The bathroom is not a good place because of severe changes in humidity and temperature that may affect shelf life. Plastic containers offer good protection and can be obtained in the easy-to-open version or the "childproof" version. Pills should never be taken from one container and placed into another one unless the prescription insert also is changed.

**Pills Should Always be Stored Out
of the Reach of Children**

COMMONLY ABUSED
PRESCRIPTION DRUGS

A few prescription drugs are widely misused. This section discusses three classifications of drugs that have a high potential for problems.

Antibiotics—Antibiotics are drugs that have been made from molds or they can be manufactured synthetically. They are highly effective in fighting infections that are caused by microorganisms other than viruses. The common cold is caused by a virus and therefore, antibiotics are ineffective in curing the cold and in relieving the symptoms. The body has natural defenses within the immune system that fight the disease.

When antibiotics are taken for the common cold, several problems arise. First, microorganisms develop mutant strains that are resistant to antibiotics, thereby rendering the drug ineffective. Secondly, antibiotics like all drugs, have side effects and the therapeutic value must be weighed against the benefits. Some individuals are allergic to antibiotics and develop an anaphylactic reaction. Finally, antibiotics destroy helpful as well as disease producing microorganisms. This may prohibit the metabolism of nutrients in food, especially some vitamins. We don't have a cure for the common cold. The best advice is to drink plenty of fluids, get adequate rest, and take aspirin, ibuprofen, or acetaminophen for the symptoms.

Anorectics—Amphetamines such as benzedrine and dexedrine are stimulants that originally were used to treat narcolepsy (sudden, uncontrollable sleep episodes). One of the side effects of these drugs is that they depress the appetite. This type of drug is called an anorectic. Because of this effect some people have used amphetamines as a weight reduction technique.

A number of problems are associated with anorectics. They increase blood pressure. In combination with dietary changes they may alter the insulin needs of diabetics. An overdose may produce confusion, panic states, depression, nausea, vomiting, and cramps. With prolonged use they may produce insomnia and other sleep disorders. Amphetamines may create an unpleasant taste in the mouth, and strangely, may produce diarrhea or constipation.

The greatest potential harm, though, is the fact that amphetamines are physically addicting. The issue, by itself, means that amphetamine prescriptions should be used sparingly. Because they produce a tolerance among users, the tendency is to increase dosage. This could create a variety of health problems. Added to the potential dangers is the fact that they are only of marginal benefit to the user. Studies have demonstrated that weight loss with amphetamines produces only a fraction of a pound difference than the same dieting program without amphetamines. Furthermore, the anorectic effect diminishes after several weeks.

Amphetamines are contraindicated for people with cardiovascular disease, hypertension, thyroid disease, and glaucoma. They should not be used by pregnant women. Many physicians would argue that anorectics should never be used as an adjunct to a weight reduction program. The best way to lose weight is to reduce calories while still eating foods within each of the four groups, to modify eating patterns, and to exercise.

Tranquilizers—Tranquilizers are safe and effective when used as prescribed and when taken over a short period of time. They are widely used to ease problems of living. Annoyances and frustrations of every day life seem less important. In other words, they help people to cope. Obviously, there is a strong tendency for psychological dependence.

In the recommended dose and over a short duration (less than four months), there is little risk of addiction. But higher doses, taken when problems seem beyond the capability of the ususal dose; or tranquilizers taken for longer periods of time, hold the serious potential for addiction. Alcohol, another drug taken in times of frustration, creates a potentiating effect with tranquilizers. These drugs impair mental and physical abilities required to perform daily tasks. Paradoxical reactions (opposite to the known therapeutic effect) have been known to occur.

In addition to the problems associated with the effects of the drug itself, tranquilizers encourage the use of drugs for immediate solutions to life situations. After swallowing the pill the individual no longer feels that the problem is quite so big. But that does nothing to resolve the issue, it only masks the symptoms. Coping is based upon self-concept and how the person perceives his/her ability to handle the situation. There is no medicine that can build one's self esteem. Anxiety and tension associated with everyday life rarely require the use of drugs. When used, tranquilizers should be under the very close supervision of a doctor.

Commonly Abused Prescription Drugs

QUESTIONS TO ASK YOUR PHYSICIAN

To get the most benefit from a prescription drug you need to communicate with your doctor. Provide him/her with as much information as you can. When the doctor asks if you are taking any other drugs be sure to consider the over-the-counter drugs and alcohol as well as prescription medicines. Make sure you clearly understand the directions for proper use, then follow the directions carefully. Some questions you need answered are listed here:

1. What is the name of the drug and how does it work?
2. When and how should I take it?
3. Does the schedule mean I must awaken during the night for a dose?
4. Are there any restrictions on activities such as driving a car or working with machinery?

5. What should I do if I miss a dose?

6. Are there any foods, drugs, or beverages that I should avoid?

7. What are the usual side effects?

8. Are there any unusual side effects that I should know about?

9. How long will I have to take the medication?

10. How should the drug be stored?

11. Do you have any samples?

12. Can you prescribe a generic name?

13. Are there any medical conditions that would prohibit the use of this drug?

Question Number 14

Gunnar G. Sevelius, M.D.

OVER-THE-COUNTER
(OTC) DRUGS

There are thousands of drug products available to consumers who hope to relieve the symptoms of minor illnesses such as indigestion, coughs due to colds, insomnia, and muscular aches and pains. Relatively few chemicals are used to formulate these trade name remedies, also called patent medicines. In order for a company to use a substance in its product, the ingredient must be both safe and effective when used as directed. These products, sold in pharmacies, supermarkets, and department stores, are known as over-the-counter drugs, often referred to as OTC.

OTC drugs are sold to relieve symptoms. In and of themselves, they do not cure disease. They simply make it easier to live with the condition. Before getting into specifics there are a few general problems associated with all over-the-counter drugs that need to be presented.

1. These products encourage self-diagnosis and self-medication. Studies show that people will choose an over-the-counter drug before seeing a doctor. In these instances, the individual assumes the role of physician. But consider coughs as an example. A cough is a natural body reflex caused by irritation. Cough syrup is capable of sedating the cough. The key issue is, "What is causing the irritation?" When the cough is due to a cold, the cough will disappear when the cold goes away. Many conditions, however, can stimulate the cough response. Some of these conditions are quite serious, and if not treated by a physician, can progress to the point where they represent a serious threat to health.

2. OTC drugs alter the body's biochemistry. These changes can reduce the effectiveness of prescription medicines; e.g, decongestants and hypertension medication. Furthermore, they can reduce the body's

ability to metabolize food and/or use the nutrients they contain.

3. OTC drugs can produce psychological dependence. If a symptom persists (because the disease is not being treated) the individual may learn to rely on the effects of the drug to induce a more comfortable state; e.g., nasal sprays. These drugs also can lead to functional dependence whenever a particular body function becomes dependent upon the use of a drug, e.g., laxatives.

Over-the-Counter (OTC)

4. OTC drugs are safe and effective when used as directed. Many people fail to read the labels or package inserts. This can lead to an incorrect dosage, an inappropriate schedule of medication, and a waste of money. Most OTC remedies say on the label, "If symptoms persist, see your physician."

5. OTC drugs often combine added ingredients that have nothing to do with the symptom in question. This is especially true of analgesics and cold remedies. Adding chemicals unnecessarily means that the body has to adjust unnecessarily. Some advertising actually promotes the issue by indicating that, "Our product has added ingredients." You should question whether these added ingredients are useful for the symptom of concern.

6. Many diseases would contraindicate the use of particular chemicals. Heart disease, kidney disease, diabetes, and glaucoma are examples. Pregnancy is another consider-ation, a pregnant woman should always check with her physician before taking an OTC product.

7. Finally, OTC drugs, in a subtle way, promote drug abuse. Americans have come to depend upon a quick and easy remedy for discomfort or displeasure without considering all of the implications. This is a dangerous behavior mode. Rather than deal with the central issue, we have come to think that relief is just a swallow away. Prescription drugs, illicit drugs, and alcohol have come to be used in the same way; e.g., tranquilizers, anorectics, marijuana, and cocaine.

Space will not permit an examination of all OTC drugs. The following section presents a few of the more commonly used preparations. Properly used, they can provide symptomatic relief, but used inappropriately they can become a threat to health.

The most commonly used products are the internal analgesics. Four compounds are widely available; aspirin, acetaminophen (Tylenol, Datril, and Panadol), ibuprofen (Nuprin and Advil) and naproxen (Aleve). Each is effective in reducing pain and lowering fever. Aspirin and ibuprofen effectively reduce inflammation. Aspirin can be a problem because some people are allergic to acetylsalicylic acid, it thins the blood, and it may cause minor gastric bleeding. Although inconclusive, aspirin has been implicated in Reyes Syndrome when given to children who have influenza or chickenpox. Ibuprofen is a lower dosage of a prescription drug sold as Motrin. The package insert indicates it should not be used by people who are allergic to aspirin, children below the age of 12, pregnant women, nursing mothers, or by people who are under medical care for any serious condition, or who are taking prescription medicines.

Manufacturers use gimmicks and clever advertising to sell additional quantities of the drug. Internal analgesics have been flavored, buffered, sugar coated, time released, combined together, and made to fizz. In the end, they are no more effective than the primary ingredient. A few examples will demonstrate how the manufacturers mislead the public.

1. Extra Strength—The therapeutic dose of aspirin is 650 mg. Extra strength, simply means more milligrams. But that would be no different than taking three regular aspirins. Extra strength does not make your pain disappear more quickly or more effectively.

2. Analgesic p.m.—A side effect of antihista-mines is to produce drowsiness. But antihistamines added to aspirin and sold OTC are so weak that this side effect is negligible. Plain aspirin before bedtime is just as effective as those with antihistamines.

3. Added Ingredients—Adding caffeine, fizz, antacids, buffering agents, timed released grains, and aspirin combined with acetaminophen raise the production

costs of the drug. These costs are passed on to the consumer with no added therapeutic effect for pain relief.

Cold Remedies—Because of the number of colds experienced annually, and the distressing nature of the combined symptoms, cold preparations are among the sales leaders in OTC drugs. Typically, they contain an internal analgesic (although occasionally in insufficient quantity to provide the therapeutic dose), a decongestant, a cough suppressant, and an antihistamine (to stop the watery eyes and runny nose). There is some legitimate question about the effectiveness of the last three ingredients. Given the benefit of the doubt, however, the real issue is that the primary benefit comes from the analgesic. If the cold remedy contains less than 650 mg per recommended dose, then the analgesic relief and lowered fever may not occur. The cold will disappear in about a week regardless of medication. The body's natural defense is the best weapon against a cold. If symptoms persist beyond a week, your physician should be consulted.

Antacids—Antacids are sold for symptomatic relief of heartburn, acid indigestion, and "sour stomach." Each of these terms is actually synonymous. The condition is caused by an excess of hydrochloric acid in the stomach. Spicy foods, alcohol, and stress can bring about the excess of hydrochloric acid. The stomach empties food content in less than an hour so the neutralizing effect of antacid is of short duration. A low pH food, like milk will serve the same effect.

The concerns with antacids are as follows: First, many people suffering from heart attacks initially self-medicate with an antacid, misdiagnosing the problem, and delaying emergency treatment. Secondly, some antacids contain aspirin, an acid. Thirdly, antacids interact with some prescription drugs, such as tetracycline, to render that drug ineffective. Fourth, antacids may constipate the person thereby encouraging the use of another OTC product. Finally, these products encourage people to treat the condition rather than to prevent it. If spicy foods, alcohol, and stress upset you, deal with cause and not the symptom.

**If You Think This is Something—Wait Until You
See the Advertising**

Laxatives—Advertisers tell us that we should have a bowel movement every day. This is not correct. The need for elimination varies and for some people (or sometimes) a bowel movement may not be needed for several days. Laxatives should have extremely limited use from a medical standpoint. Because constipation can be caused by inadequate fluid intake, lack of fibers in the diet, lack of physical exercise, and stress, these issues should be examined before resorting to a laxative.

Many problems are associated with laxatives. They so thoroughly cleanse the bowel that another elimination may not be necessary for several days. But this encourages succeeding use of the drug. It is possible to become functionally dependent upon laxatives, where the bowel needs stimulation for peristalsis. Laxatives can produce dehydration, depletion of minerals, elevation of blood pressure, electrolyte imbalance, and may complicate existing diseases. Constipation is a symptom, not a disease. Again, the source of the problem should be treated rather than the symptom.

Briefly, some additional OTC drug concerns are:

Sleep aids—Actually disturb the sleep pattern and reduce the amount of dream (deep) sleep.

Nasal sprays—Create a rebound effect where the nasal passages are opened but when the effect wears off the membranes swell worse than they were before using the drug.

Eyewashes—Gets the red out but are not as effective as the natural tear process. Eyewashes can interfere with the production of tears.

Mouthwashes—Temporarily will kill bacteria but cannot cure an infection in the nose, throat, ear, or mouth that produces the odor.

External analgesics—Irritate the skin, can become toxic with prolonged use, and are incapable of penetrating the muscle where the real source of the problem lies.

Hemorrhoidals—No evidence exists that these products substantially shrink the swelling. They contain a topical anesthetic which works for a short period of time, but in no way do these products heal the condition. Use may delay examination and treatment of a more serious condition.

In summary, OTC drugs are sold for the symptomatic relief of minor conditions. They are generally safe and effective when used as directed.

Certain conditions such as diabetes, arthritis, kidney disease, heart disease, thyroid disease, peptic ulcer, and cancer may prevent the use of some drugs. Pregnant women should always check with their doctor. Whenever symptoms persist, see your doctor. Over-the-counter drugs may need to be discontinued several days before surgery since they may affect the administration of anesthetics or the surgery itself. Finally, be aware of any behavior change after taking drugs. It may be the result of the drug.

Caffeine—Because caffeine is the most widely used drug in America a brief discussion is warranted. Caffeine, present in many over-the-counter drugs, reduces drowsiness and fatigue. It is a central nervous system stimulant that is found in coffee, tea, coca, and cola drinks.

Caffeine poses a number of health-related concerns. For one thing, it is capable of producing physical dependence. Prolonged users may experience withdrawal symptoms that include headache, nausea, anxiety, tension, and irritability. Many people with emotional problems rely on caffeine, which only makes the situation worse because a progressive cycle is established.

Caffeine has other serious negative effects. It produces sleep disturbances and the user may find it difficult to fall asleep. It constricts the blood vessels, while at the same time it stimulates the stress hormones. This results in more blood trying to get through smaller vessels, thereby increasing heart rate and blood pressure. In laboratory animals excessive quantities of caffeine have produced birth defects and delayed skeletal development of the fetus. Although these results may not be the same in humans, there is enough scientific question to recommend that pregnant women use caffeine sparingly. The cardiovascular, kidney, and emotional changes brought about by caffeine are sufficiently important to reinforce this recommendation.

SUMMARY

In summary, drugs can be helpful and they can be harmful. It is a matter of fitting the dose to the person's need considering the person's size, age, sensitivity and attitude toward the drug. As this is an intricate balance, it is in everyone's interest to know the basic drug facts presented in this text. It is particularly important for those persons with chronic conditions requiring the use of the drugs for a long period of time to know their action and interaction with other drugs and foods.

The human body is a delicate self-regulating machine which requires good maintenance and our support so that we can add years to our life and life to our years perhaps a hundred or more.

ALCOHOL

Minimizing Your Risk of

Alcoholism, the Completely Unnecessary Disease

G. Sevelius, M.D.

Drunkenness... spoils health, dismounts
the mind, and unmans men.

William Penn (1644 - 1718)

INTRODUCTION

Fermentation of carbohydrates or various sugars produces alcohol. Like all foreign chemical substances or drugs, alcohol has a wide range of pharmacological actions in the human body. These actions differ with length of use and quantities consumed. In humans, the short and long-term effects of alcohol are mostly on the nervous system, including the brain, and on the digestive organs, particularly the liver.

Throughout history, almost every culture has made use of the pleasurable effects of alcohol. In our society's forms of social interaction, alcoholic beverages are ever present. Alcohol causes some pleasant effects, but also has some health risks. As with practically anything we consume, excessive use of alcohol is destructive.

Due to the availability of better statistics and advanced research in recent years, we have changed our views on human behavior toward weight, smoking, exercise, and several other health areas to prevent harm to our bodies. It is only natural that we also examine the use of alcohol.

This chapter provides information about alcohol, alcohol use, and alcohol abuse.

DEFINITIONS

Understanding four basic definitions will create a framework for reference while studying this text.

1) NON-DRINKER:	One who does not drink at all, or may have a maximum of one to two drinks per year.
2) SOCIAL DRINKER:	One who drinks more or less steadily, but at a predictable rate, with no major volume increase or decrease relative to the passage of time. This predictable rate may run from two to three drinks per week to one to two drinks per day.
3) ALCOHOL ABUSER:	One who severely abuses alcohol on isolated, single occasions. This individual could die of alcohol abuse or become a highway fatality, but this is not the disease of alcoholism.
4) ALCOHOLIC:	One whose continuous use of alcohol affects all major areas of life, including personal health, finance, and interper-sonal relationships.
	One who, after the first drink, is not able to predict his or her behavior.
	One whose rate of alcohol consumption varies with large swings. This is the behavioral disease of alcoholism.

STATISTICS

Alcoholics comprise five percent of the total population—ten million people. National surveys reveal that 50 percent of the U.S. population older than 15 years of age drink alcohol occasionally. What was once considered a male-dominated disease now affects both sexes equally. Alcoholism is also rapidly becoming a major health hazard for children. These ten million alcoholics are responsible for:

- 45 percent of all hospital admissions
- 25 percent of all attempted suicides
- 39 percent of all broken marriages
- 50 percent of all traffic arrests
- 50 percent of all fatal automobile accidents, with loss of 25,000 lives annually
- 25 percent loss of employee productivity.

Aside from loss of life and personal tragedies, the above statistics carry an enormous price tag. It is estimated that this tag is as large as our total defense budget.

The extent of the effects of alcohol in terms of financial loss and disrupted lives is totally beyond comprehension. Without comparison, either socially or medically, alcoholism is the most expensive disease in our nation. Ironically, alcoholism is an unnecessary disease.

CULTURAL BACKGROUND

Almost all cultures through the ages have used alcoholic beverages to promote fellowship. The introduction of alcohol into a group made individuals approachable. The same is true for modern society. Friendships and business associates are often started at parties where alcoholic beverages are facilitators in bringing strangers together. Alcohol diminishes tension, a role that is an important part of our very mobile society. All through history, people have recognized what alcohol can do for them.

Trouble starts when individuals drink alcohol and do not realize what it does to them. This is one of the differences between social drinking and alcoholism. Winston Churchill said it well: "Always remember... that I have taken more out of alcohol than alcohol has taken out of me."

The purpose of this chapter is to give a warning to those who might have slipped into a "too much" habit. Too much of something can spoil anything, and too much alcohol can spoil a good party as well as a human life.

Here I will deviate from the original manuscript, originally written for a specific working population.

What I would call "social drug use" has been a facilitator in social get togethers or celebrations in all of human history. Abuse is usually taking place in a setting of social isolation instead of with friends. As the medical director for a large aerospace industry, I found that self-destructive use of alcohol occurred in less than one percent of our working population.

Behind each single number of abuse usage is most often hiding a family tragedy. Realizing that such family tragedies do occur, I must still recognize the larger picture. From the standpoint of the whole society, all through history, no society has broken down from individual abuse of social drug use. In modern time, with medical cost covered by insurance, we do know that the abuse of social drugs costs the society a considerable amount of money, but also that tax on the products they use are able to pay for their abuse, their own treatment, and for the preventive education of the general public.

Laws on social drugs are instituted for the purpose of what the public perceives is the best for their families. Such laws have to be democratically based. My proposal here has to be taken only as my own personal opinion. I decided to publish my opinion because it is based on my somewhat unique experience as a medical physician of a large working population and my recent studies of 200,000 years of world history and five world religions: "The Nine Pillars of History." (www.ninepillars.com)

My reason for joining groups of people who are proposing a radical change in public policy is based on the following:

1) You, and only you, are responsible for your own health habits.

2) Society is responsible for the education of the risk and consequences of different health habits.

3) The family, school and free press are responsible for transferring the knowledge of the consequences of health habits.

4) Family tradition, social behavior, religion and the obvious destructive results from abuse are strong antidotes for most people.

5) Religion and recovered abusers can help in creating a supportive fellowship, watching out for the consequences of poor health habits.

6) There is no epidemic abuse, despite easy access to social drugs, in countries that are heavily involved with the production of these elsewhere illegal drugs.

7) I do not see why an epidemic abuse would take over in highly educated societies.

8) No free nation in history has succumbed to an epidemic use of social drugs. The attempt to regulate the sale of alcohol in the U.S. and in many other western nations in the twenties and thirties stands as a warning example. The time saw raging Mafia-like wars for earnings outside tax control. Laws regulating social drug use are totally naïve and unenforceable.

Any attempt to control social drugs has resulted in an underground industry that does not care about the consequences of an individual's health or for the consequences of leaving out

Gunnar G. Sevelius, M.D.

taxes from the social equation. At present, this is what is taking place in the U.S. and in many modern industrialized nations. Such countries continuously bleed from the lack of taxes from the underground promotion of marijuana and "harder drugs" such as opium derivatives. Instead, earnings from producing and selling social drugs is supporting organized Mafia-like organizations or even non-national militia gangs with the sole purpose of destructing or derailing the law-abiding societies to which they sell their drugs. Youth involved in distributing these "illegal" drugs fill our jails or kill each other on the streets instead of doing constructive work in the society and partake in the taxpaying equation for common good.

In short, legislative law should concentrate on enforcing individual support and education for good personal habits; not trying to control "illegal" drug distribution, an impossible task.

MEDICAL EFFECTS OF ALCOHOL INTAKE

A. ACUTE EFFECTS

Small doses of 90-proof alcohol, one or two ounces, stimulate cardiac output (the amount of blood the heart pumps per minute), giving the individual an extra boost of energy. Along with this increase in energy, the individual's mood is elevated, creating a feeling of lightheartedness. At the same time, inhibiting reflexes in the brain tend to relax—particularly those of social restraint. After two or three ounces, a depressing effect on the brain shadows all other effects. The individual's behavior becomes more and more childish, with moods often shifting from happy to sad in minutes. After four or five ounces, a large number of the brain cells have become toxic or disconnected. Reflexes become slow, speech slurred, walk unsteady, and all thought processes are self-centered and irrational. After eight or ten ounces, the individual usually falls asleep or becomes unconscious. At this point, without a developed tolerance, a person could die. Recovering from binges of one week or longer, the individual may have hallucinations and great anxiety (delirium tremens) when the brain cells return to normal or start to "come together" again.

An individual is considered under the influence and legally prohibited from operating a motor vehicle if the alcohol content of the blood is 80 milligrams of alcohol to 100 milliliters of blood. In medical terms, this is the same as 0.08 percent (8 promille) blood alcohol.

Gunnar G. Sevelius, M.D.

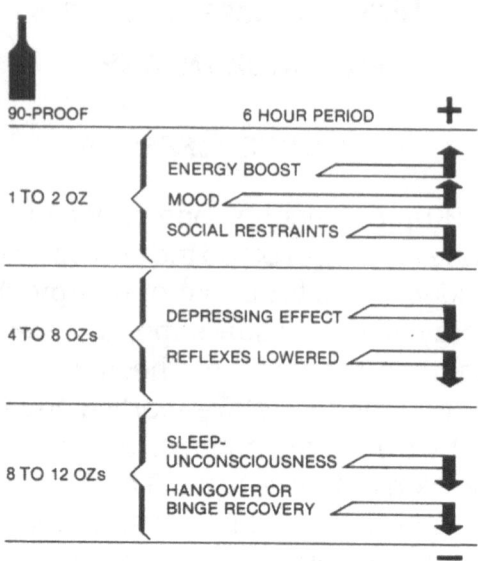

The effects on behavior are related to blood alcohol concentration as follows:

0.03 percent = Slightly elevated mood
0.05 percent = Mild mental incoordination
0.10 percent = Staggering walk
0.20 percent = Slurred and repetitive speech, loss of ability to balance
0.30 percent = Recognizable incoordinated speech and muscular contractions
0.40 percent = Sleep, nonresponsive to stimuli
0.50 percent = Lethal to 50 percent of individ-uals (death is due mainly to the toxic effect of alcohol on life support centers in the brain).

Each ounce of 100-proof whiskey (50 percent alcohol) raises the blood level approximately 0.02 percent in a 170-pound person. The same effect can be reached with wine or beer. Wine usually consists of 12 percent alcohol, and beer has four to six percent alcohol (each requiring correspondingly larger quantities to cause the same effect as 50 percent alcohol—four times the quantity for wine and five times for beer). This does not hinder an individual from becoming as intoxicated on wine or beer as with 80 or 90-proof liquor. Advanced age, weight loss, medical conditions, slowed circulation or metabolism, and tranquilizing drugs can make an individual more sensitive to alcohol.

B. Chronic Effects

It is a well-known fact that alcohol mixes with both water and fat. Alcohol, after ingestion, diffuses into just about every cell in the body—except possibly the cartilage and bone. Chronic alcohol abuse can and will affect every cell and organ function of the body. The most striking effects are in the brain and the liver.

Alcohol and the Brain

The brain works much like a computer—with fewer memory cells it works more slowly. The acute effect of alcohol is to temporarily disconnect the nerve cells in the brain. This effect is made permanent by chronic alcohol usage. Memory blackouts and early senility from chronic alcohol abuse are characteristic for an alcoholic. Because the individual's own brain is affected, the alcoholic cannot recognize the personality change that is taking place. Typically, a well-educated person is able to carry on a relatively rational conversation about the weather and wind, but is unable to solve simple mathematical problems.

ALCOHOL AND THE LIVER

The most well known medical effect of chronic alcohol abuse is the effect on the liver. The liver contains an enzyme, alcohol dehydrogenase (an enzyme is a chemical that promotes a chemical reaction just by its presence) that breaks up the alcohol so the body can burn alcohol just as it burns simple sugar. This creates extra calories and leads to extra pounds of fat, first in the liver and later throughout the body. Each liver cell can become so engorged with fat that the liver can double in size. Such an enlarged liver might be felt three or four inches below the rib cage in the upper right abdomen.

Fat-engorged liver cells don't work well and can unintentionally release enzymes into the bloodstream. Common enzymes and other blood tests can indicate disturbed liver cell functions through elevated blood concentrations of:

Normal Range (units):

- SGOT (Serum glutamic oxaloacetic transaminase)   (5-50)
- SGPT (Serum glutamic pyruvic transaminase)   (0-40)
- GGPT (Gamma glutamic pyruvic

transaminase)   (0-42)

- Uric acid   (3- 9)

The level in one or more of these tests is usually elevated in alcohol liver disease. The GGPT test is said to be the most sensitive.

The growth of liver cells enlarged by fat can be reversed. The body will use the stored fat in the cells as fuel if the alcohol intake is stopped. The liver, and most of its cells, will then return to normal size and function.

Liver cells will burst like over-inflated balloons if high alcohol intake is continued. When this occurs, the liver cells are replaced by fibrous scar tissue, and the liver shrinks to an uneven, hard mass. The medical term for this condition is liver cirrhosis.

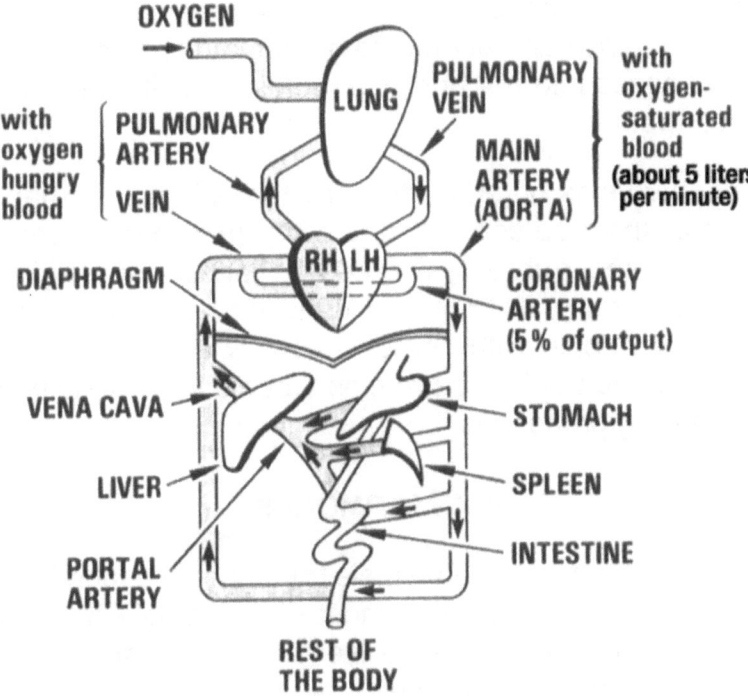

One of the main functions of the liver is to filter blood from the stomach, intestine, and spleen before it enters the general circulation. The veins from these organs join together to form a large portal vein joining the liver from its underside. The blood from the portal vein is fed into liver capillaries. Toxic substances and foreign substances are filtered and chemically altered by enzymes in the liver cells. The blood is again collected on the top side of the liver in a large vein called the vena cava, which empties blood into the heart. All the blood in the vena cava should be compatible with the body as a result of the treatment it has received in the liver.

Portal circulation averages one quart of blood per minute, or about 20 percent of the total cardiac output. This large amount of blood flow demands resistance-free passage throughout the liver. The passage will become blocked if the liver is scarred by cirrhosis. The organs that return venous blood through the liver (the stomach, intestine, and spleen) become engorged with backed-up blood. Large hemorrhoids are an early symptom of this problem. The pressure in the capillaries from these engorged organs can become so great that the fluid portion of the blood oozes into the body's abdominal cavity causing the infamous "beer belly."

At times, the veins burst, particularly those in the stomach or esophagus (the tube connecting the mouth with the stomach). This can cause life-threatening hemorrhages that are difficult to reach surgically. This critical condition is complicated by the fact that people with cirrhosis usually also suffer from a low concentration of blood proteins that aid in the clotting and natural healing processes.

SEX HORMONES

Everyone has both male and female hormones produced in their body. The male liver destroys most of the female hormones, mostly estrogen, and the female liver destroys most of the male hormones, mostly testosterone.

With chronic alcohol abuse, the liver becomes so distorted that it filters out the body's own sex hormones and allows a build-up in sex hormones of the opposite sex. Alcoholic males tend to develop enlarged breasts and shrunken testicles from the female hormones circulating in their system. This can lead to impotence. Alcoholic females tend to develop deepened voices, male hair growth, and become asexual (no interest in sex). The characteristic alcoholic red nose, red palms, and withered muscles are also a sign of abnormal metabolism of sex hormones. Fortunately, most of these abnormal liver functions are reversible if alcohol abuse has not caused moderate or advanced cirrhosis.

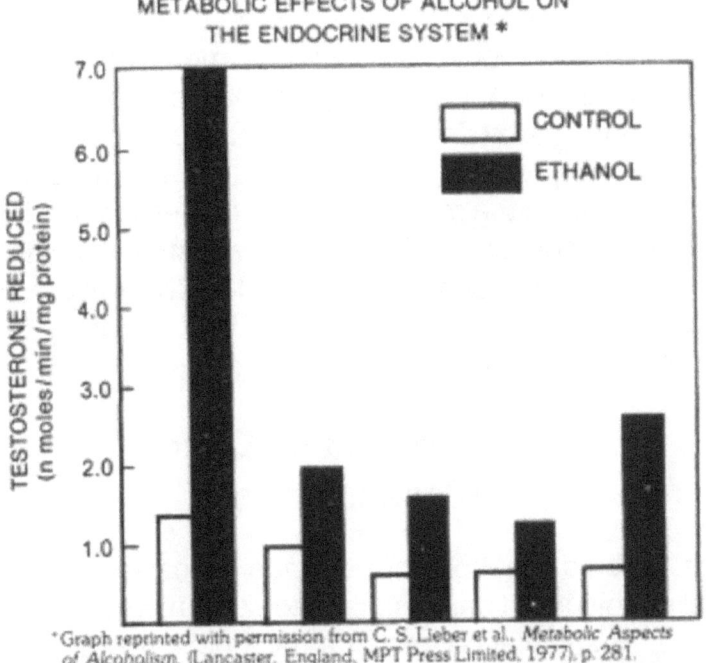

METABOLIC EFFECTS OF ALCOHOL ON
THE ENDOCRINE SYSTEM *

*Graph reprinted with permission from C. S. Lieber et al., *Metabolic Aspects of Alcoholism.* (Lancaster. England, MPT Press Limited, 1977), p. 281.

*Graph reprinted with permission from C.S.Lieber et al., *Metabolic Aspects of Alcoholism,* **(Lancaster, England, MPT Press Limited, 1977), p.281**

The increase in destruction of male sex hormones in five volunteers after 28 days of high alcohol intake is indicated by the dark bars on the chart.

Premature Death

Premature death (occurring from age 50 or 60 or perhaps earlier) is ten times more common for the alcoholic than for the non-alcoholic. The reason for premature death can come from complications of liver disease, injuries due to accidents, or even suicide. Many people believe alcoholism to be a slow suicide in itself. The young alcoholic will deny any suicide thoughts. However, the older alcoholic is mentally, physically, and socially so depressed and debilitated that an end to his suffering is a relieving thought.

Pregnancy

A special warning should be given to women who drink alcohol during pregnancy. A growing fetus has an extremely high metabolic rate (as evidenced by the growth from one cell to a newborn baby within nine months). The fetus sucks any available food from the mother's placenta—including alcohol, if present in the mother's blood. Alcohol will affect all cells of the fetus—especially the sensitive brain cells. Children of alcoholic mothers have a 50 percent chance of being mentally retarded ("fetal alcohol syndrome").

Social Effects of Chronic Alcohol Abuse

Just as chronic alcohol abuse leads to certain predictable medical conditions, it can also lead to certain predictable social situations. The social pattern of an alcoholic is directly related to two fundamental facts—dependence on money and time.

Liquor in large amounts is expensive. Unfortunately, chronic alcoholics often allow other financial obligations to take a second place to their drinking needs. Most alcoholics have financial problems, and for many the economic burden of constantly buying alcohol leads to poverty. In desperation, the alcoholic will sometimes resort to theft.

Most people divide their time relatively equally between work, family, and sleep. The alcohol habit requires time to indulge and recover. Employers will not allow employees to be under the influence of alcohol on the job. Because alcohol is a sedative, more hours are needed for sleep. Therefore, the time for the family is affected first and most. Carrying both the financial burden and the time burden of the alcohol habit, the family of the alcoholic often suffers more than the alcoholic himself.

NORMAL SOCIAL PATTERN

ALCOHOLIC SOCIAL PATTERN

Eventually, the alcohol habit will extend its influence to the work schedule. First, the alcoholic will not show up at work on Fridays or Mondays. He will exhibit behavior changes, poor judgment, unpredict-ability, and unreliability. Later, as the disease becomes more severe, the alcoholic risks being under the influence while at work, covering up the odor with strong mouthwash and mints. Most alcoholics don't realize that their problem is known to fellow employees. Many are not reported because of "buddy solidarity." This buddy solidarity can lead to late treatment of the alcoholic—often too late to save his job, his family, and sometimes his life. This cover-up is demonstrated by both family members and fellow employees; it is referred to as "killing with kindness."

DRINKING VERSUS DRIVING

There are approximately 50,000 fatalities resulting from automobile accidents each year in the United States. Almost half, or 20,000, of these are attributed to drunk drivers. We can probably conservatively assume that about half of these (approximately 12,500) are innocent victims killed by the drunk driver. This statistic makes the alcoholic the most likely person in society to commit homicide—even more likely than someone owning a hand gun. It is one good reason for the growing movement across the country to stiffen penalties for driving under the influence. The chronic alcoholic typically has two or more drunk driving violations. Driving violations are perhaps as valid as any medical test in defining an alcoholic.

FAMILY OF THE ALCOHOLIC BREADWINNER

Insecurity is the one word that best defines the life of a family dependent upon an alcoholic. Promises of emotional and financial support are often broken in order to support the alcohol habit. The family can never really be sure what will or could happen in the next hour. Hundreds of questions fill the minds of the alcoholic's family—questions like "Will he come home safely tonight?", "Will he spend time with us this weekend?", or "Will she lose her job?".

Children raised in an alcoholic household tend to mature earlier than other children, due in part to the tragedy they are forced to witness every day. Many children try to find their own security through early independence. Many others turn to alcohol abuse themselves, imitating "adult" images.

WOMEN AND ALCOHOL

Alcoholism was once thought of as a male-oriented disease. With more women entering a once male-dominated industrial workforce and achieving financial independence, more are being recognized as alcoholics. Social isolation and early signs of liver disease, although typical for any alcoholic, appear to surface sooner in women. It also appears that early statistics showing only 25 percent of our society's alcoholics as women were invalid due to an inaccurate sampling. Women were protected by the sanctity of the home and many alcoholics were not identified by these studies. Evidence now holds that the disease of alcoholism is evenly spread between males and females.

RETIRED PERSONS AND ALCOHOL

As the body grows older, its metabolism slows down, decreasing the amount of alcohol (or any drug) needed to reach specific levels of intoxication. An intake level that might be socially acceptable for a young person with a high metabolic rate can cause marked intoxication in an older person.

The brain recharges itself during normal sleep by fluctuating patterns of activity alternating between deep and light sleep, about three or four fluctuations per night. As we get older, it is very common to wake up during the light sleep periods. It is a common misbelief that these wake-up periods are harmful, destroying the next day's activities. This misunderstanding has produced widespread anxiety about sleep, causing many people to use all kinds of sleeping aids. Some use alcohol in large doses to induce sleep because it is available without a prescription.

The brain, however, will not recharge in the normal fluctuating pattern after alcohol or most sleeping pills. Although the person "slept" throughout the night, he will wake up just as tired as when he went to sleep—often with added anxiety, depression, and hangover headaches caused by the alcohol or pills. An elderly person needs to be very cautious with both alcohol and medications because of a decreased tolerance due to age.

SYNERGISM

Synergism is a term used to express the enhanced medical effect that often occurs when two drugs are taken together and both act in a similar fashion on the metabolic system in the body. As I mentioned earlier, alcohol is a sedative—it slows down the activities of the nervous system. Sleeping pills are also sedatives. If one sedative unit of alcohol is added to one sedative unit of a sleeping pill, the medical effect on the nervous system will not be two sedative units but more like three. It is very easy to overdose the body by mixing drugs—even if the consumption of each one by itself does not appear to be a dangerous amount. Drugs that have synergistic effects with alcohol include sleeping pills, tran-quilizers, most antihistamines, and most illicit drugs. The warning should be made again that age, fatigue, diet, and many heart and metabolic diseases may further enhance synergistic action between drugs.

DIAGNOSIS OF ALCOHOLISM

Alcoholism is a disease of denial... denial that drinking harms the body, mind, and social lifestyle—even when facts to the contrary are overwhelming. The rationalization that takes place in the mind of an alcoholic has been figuratively characterized by recovered alcoholics as "stinking thinking." This stinking thinking is what makes the disease of alcoholism so difficult for the alcoholic to recognize. Failure to recognize the problem delays the process of identification and treatment (a fatal Catch 22!).

"I only had two beers!"

Alcoholism can affect anyone. It is a disease not related to age, sex, education, religion, income, or cultural background. Slight statistical preponderance in any one group only serves to prejudice judgment of uninvolved people and has no medical or social value. Once the alcohol abuse habit has started, both medical and social signs will repeat—no matter who or when it hits.

The following are symptoms and signs of an alcoholic, listed in order from early to late.

A. SOCIAL SYMPTOMS

- Gulping instead of sipping alcohol
- Starting arguments with family while under the influence
- Friends commenting on changed personality
- Continuous drinking until the bottle is empty
- Borrowing money to buy alcohol
- Drinking alone or in hiding
- Two or more drunk-driving violations
- Family threatening to break up
- Supervisor complaining about poor performance or attendance at work

B. MEDICAL SYMPTOMS AND SIGNS

- Elevated blood concentrations of liver enzymes
- Memory blackouts
- Impotence—sexual dysfunction; this affects both sexes
- Anemia
- Engorged abdominal organs and large hemorrhoids
- Cirrhosis of the liver with signs of blood flow congestion
- Loss of memory
- Tingling sensations in the legs
- Flushed nose and palms
- Withering muscle tissues
- Central nervous system damage, including tremors, anxiety, and poor hand-to-eye coordination

People with these trouble signs have varying degrees of alcoholism. Severe alcoholics will show more symptoms than weekend abusers or heavy drinkers. However, all these people need help and treatment to overcome their disease.

Gunnar G. Sevelius, M.D.

TREATMENT OF ALCOHOLISM

Alcoholism is a disease of behavior. The diseased behavior is a denial linked to alcohol. Successful treatment has to start with breaking the link between alcohol and denial. Thereafter, sobriety can be supported by different enhancements. Alcohol affects the brain so the link between "denial" and "alcohol" cannot be seen by the alcoholic himself. Even while sober, the alcoholic brain either forgets or denies the link between alcohol and any of its consequences. The most effective time to approach an alcoholic is when he is in a high anxiety state, right after from a binge during which he has been hurt mentally, physically, socially, or economically. Such an approach should be supported by accurate recover-ing documentation to counteract the alcoholic's well-honed denial system. Recovered alcoholics call this "bottoming-out." The alcoholic must realize that alcohol and bottoming-out are directly related. The connection between alcohol and the painful consequence must be truly undeniable. This offers a base for a commitment to stop drinking. Any options to continue the habit are compromises. All compromises are stinking thinking and part of the denial behavior. A compromise in a bottoming-out situation will always fail.

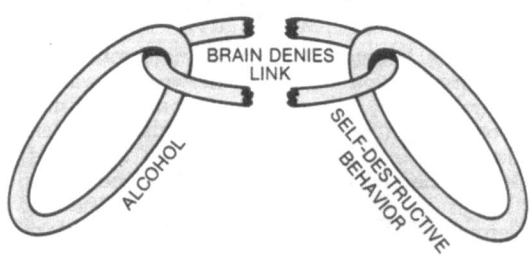

ALCOHOLICS ANONYMOUS

Alcoholics Anonymous (AA) is a non-profit, voluntary organization of men and women with an alcoholic history. These men and women have gone through what they call "every stinking thinking theme that an alcoholic can dream up" before their denial behavior bottomed-out and they sought help through AA. All of the members have devoted themselves to a life free from alcohol and to helping those alcoholics who are asking for help. The experience and insight the AA member can bring into a counseling session with an alcoholic is always extremely impressive to the alcoholic. It makes the alcoholic recognize the link between hurting and denial of the alcohol as the culprit. This is the beginning of the road to recovery. The AA organization will give the self-admitted alcoholic a supportive environment to continue a life free from alcohol.

AA meetings are held in almost every town across the United States on several nights each week. The Alcoholics Anonymous telephone number is listed in the white pages of any phone book. There is only one requirement for help—you have to go to AA, they will not come to you. Counseling is voluntary, free, and completely confidential. To join AA is to make a commitment to sobriety, and to later help and counsel the newest members of AA. Continued counseling strengthens the alcoholic's commitment to sobriety. The AA program is essentially a support fellowship in which each member tries to uphold the twelve steps of AA:

THE AA PRAYER*

1. *We admitted we were powerless over alcohol— that our lives had become unmanageable.*

2. *We came to believe that a Power greater than ourselves could restore us to sanity.*

3. *We made a decision to turn our will and our lives over to the care of God as we understood Him.*

4. *We made a searching and fearless moral inventory of ourselves.*

5. *We admitted to God, to ourselves, and to another human being the exact nature of our wrongs.*

6. *We were entirely ready to have God remove all these defects of character.*

7. *We humbly asked Him to remove our shortcomings.*

8. *We made a list of all persons we had harmed, and became willing to make amends to them all.*

9. *We made direct amends to such people wherever possible, except when to do so would injure them or others.*

10. *We continued to take personal inventory, and when we were wrong, promptly admitted it.*

11. *We sought through prayer and meditation to improve our conscious contact with God as we understood Him, praying only for knowledge of His will for us and the power to carry that out.*

12. *We had a spiritual awakening as the result of these steps, and tried to carry this message to alcoholics, and to practice these principles in all our affairs.*

*The Twelve Steps reprinted with permission of Alcoholics Anonymous World Services, Inc. © 1939.

The Higher Power can be a religious entity or just a sublime entity to whom the alcoholic admits power-lessness towards alcohol. The fellowship of AA is one way to reinforce a commitment to sobriety.

Another widely used method is the prescription of Antabuse, a drug taken in the morning that induces vomiting if alcohol is ingested at anytime during the day. Under a doctor's supervision in some treatment centers, the alcoholic purposely takes Antabuse with a small amount of alcohol to develop an aversion toward alcohol.

Group therapy, under the leadership of a specially-trained psychologist, is another method of treatment. The group acts out the stinking thinking scenario, thereby acknowledging it. Different treatments can be carried out in special institutions or on an outpatient basis.

There is no best treatment for everyone. Treatments can be as diverse as the disease itself. A variety of options are necessary to handle a disease that affects so many different personality types. The AA organization and the counseling given by its members is, by far, the most readily available and most successful mode of treating alcoholism. Alcoholics who have been successfully treated by AA number in the millions. Most professional treatment centers will, to some degree, rely on Alcoholics Anonymous. Continuing therapy is very necessary.

THE ROLE OF INDUSTRY

The employer of an alcoholic is in control of the financial support of the alcoholic habit—the salary. The employer can also control the treatment through medical insurance coverage. Many of today's major employers recognize alcoholism as a disease and will help the alcoholic with company-financed treatment programs.

One way to start a company program for the treatment of alcoholism is to form an "Action Committee on Alcoholism." This committee should be composed of AA members—both male and female, salaried and hourly employees. The purpose of the committee is to counsel co-workers in need of treatment. If, within a short time, the entire staff is completely occupied with counseling sessions, they should be able to convince the company to hire a full-time counselor.

The counselor can be selected from within the group or can be a professional. Today, most professional counselors have had special training and certification. In either case, the counselor should have the trust of the committee. A counselor selected in this way will quickly win support from both management and employees. Thereafter, company policies and agreements with unions are greatly facilitated.

Many companies have the policy of firing an employee who has been identified as an alcoholic by poor performance on the job. This could be viewed as a disciplinary rule, but this should not be the purpose. The rule should be viewed as a medical prescription or a prescribed bottoming-out to save the life and career of an otherwise excellent employee. The rule should be used with an option for the employee to reapply for employment, with appropriate seniority, if the employee shows that positive steps have been taken toward a life of sobriety. The earlier this occurs, the greater the chances are for recovery from the disease. A warning: just signing up for counseling without personal commitment will not accomplish sobriety and will not protect the employee from judgment of workmanship.

Companies with formal alcohol programs can expect about 0.1 to 0.2 percent of their work force to need assistance each month. Twenty-five percent of these employees will be referred by supervisors, but 75 percent will volunteer themselves. The success rate of such a company program can be expected to be about 70 to 80 percent. Those who do not return to work do so because they choose to support their disease by an independent source, like retirement or another job. All those who volunteer for treatment must be handled with the utmost confidentiality and should be under no threat of losing their jobs for having volunteered. Instead, efforts towards sobriety should be supported by all available means.

Recovered employees are thankful afterward—not only for their jobs, but also for their lives. An alcoholic who is sober is characteristically a very warm and devoted person. Returning this person to a productive life creates a loyal and valuable employee.

"We're all together again!"

Company alcohol programs have grown into what is now called Employee Assistance Programs (EAP). This recognizes that an employee's productivity is not only related to his own problems, but also can be related to those of the employee's family.

Today, a denial behavior is not only linked to alcohol—it can be linked to a whole myriad of drugs, both legal and illegal. No matter what the cause, the problem has to be dealt with in an open and rational manner by those in responsible positions.

SUMMARY

To the physician, alcoholism is a treatable disease of metabolic failure; to the alcoholic, alcoholism is a disease of behavior. The behavior is a denial of the link between alcohol and self-destructiveness. Once the denial pattern has started, alcoholism is usually on its way. A list of medical and social signs can confirm the diagnosis. About five percent of the total population past the age of puberty is afflicted by alcoholism. It is one of the most costly and detrimental medical conditions in our society. Still, the disease can be controlled if the patient submits to treatment. A cure from alcoholism will add years to your life, and life to your and your family's years.

AIDS AND HIV DISEASE

Gunnar Sevelius, M.D.

The AIDS disease is the most urgent health problem in the United States of America.

Margaret Heckler

Secretary of Health 1983 - 1985

INTRODUCTION

In 1981 Dr. Abrams diagnosed several cases of a disease called Kaposi's sarcoma. This is such an unusual disease that it is surprising if the same doctor sees more than one case a year. In addition, Kaposi's sarcoma is a disease of old men. Here were seven to eight cases being seen by Dr. Abrams at the same time and they were all from young males. Dr. Abrams was intrigued and went to his colleagues and reported that he thought there was a small epidemic underway. This was one of the first manifestations of the AIDS problem in San Francisco. Dr. Abrams has stayed with the AIDS program and has become one of the nation's prominent educators on the subject.

It has been a privilege for us to have the assistance of Dr. Abrams in developing this chapter about AIDS and related conditions. It is our hope that it will bring about better understanding of this complex disease and help control its further spread. The company became the first large organization to accept AIDS-positive employees in its workforce.

HIV AND AIDS

AIDS (Acquired Immune Deficiency Syndrome) is a disease that was first widely recognized in the U.S.A. in 1981. Since its discovery, deaths due to AIDS have doubled every nine months. By July 1987, six years after it was first recognized, there were 20,000 deaths reported due to AIDS in the U.S.A. alone.

A major worldwide research effort is underway to learn more about the disease, how to control it and how to treat it. Much has been learned. One of the most important of the discoveries is that the AIDS syndrome is only one of several stages of an infection caused by a virus now identified as the Human Immunodeficiency Virus (HIV). The virus has been identified as a so-called retrovirus. In this chapter, we will call the disease from the Immune Deficiency Virus the HIV disease or HIV infection, and with this name we will refer to all of its stages, including AIDS. It is estimated that one and a half million young people in the United States are now infected with the virus. For simplicity, we will identify four individual stages of the HIV infection.

STAGE I: INCUBATION AND GROWTH

The incubation stage, in some cases, is charac-terized by the affected individual having a flu-like disease six to eight weeks after exposure. More often, however, there are no specific symptoms. If symptoms such as fever, weakness, and muscle ache are present, they tend to last longer than a seasonal flu. Typical exposure involves contact with contaminated blood or sexual fluids. The person will have the virus in the body but will not yet have had time to form antibodies against the virus. The person is contagious and can spread the virus through sexual contact, blood donation, or infected hypodermic needles.

The incubation period may or may not be followed by a heavy viral proliferation stage characterized by swollen lymph nodes in the neck, armpit, or groin. When present, these nodes can be felt almost almond size under the skin. The person may experience weight loss, feel weak, have irregular fevers, night sweats, and diarrhea lasting for several days or weeks. During this stage the virus has invaded most lymph organs, the spleen, thymus, and bone marrow.

During this growth period, the patient has plenty of virus in the body and can spread the disease by sexual contact or blood transfer. By now, antibodies have formed against the virus, so blood tests are positive.

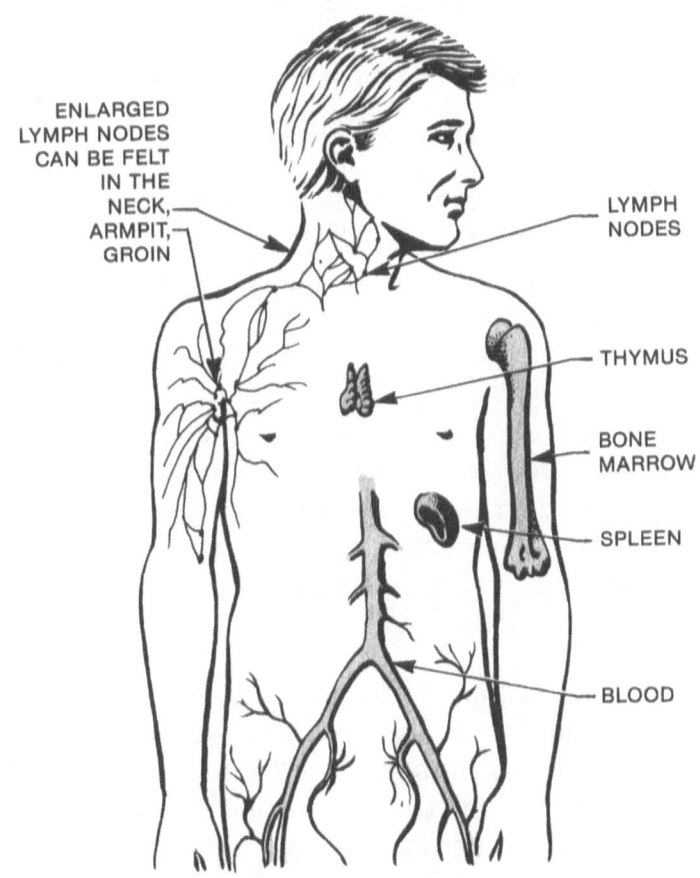

ENLARGED LYMPH NODES CAN BE FELT IN THE NECK, ARMPIT, GROIN

LYMPH NODES

THYMUS

BONE MARROW

SPLEEN

BLOOD

The Immune System

STAGE II: BALANCED STAGE
ASYMPTOMATIC

The balanced stage is characterized by an apparently healthy individual who has gone through Stage I, with or without symptoms, but whose antibody system has survived and actually reached an equilibrium with the HIV virus. The virus is still present, but the immune system has fought the virus invasion to an apparent standoff. The patient feels healthy. Only laboratory signs such as positive tests for blood antibodies reveal the presence of infection. The patient is able to transmit the virus through sex or blood transfers.

STAGE III: BALANCED STAGE ARC (AIDS-RELATED COMPLEX)

In Stage III, the patient, as in Stage II, is at a standoff with the virus invasion but does have enlarged lymph nodes as a sign of an ongoing disease. The individual is, however, feeling well. Enlarged lymph nodes can be felt in the groin, armpit, and on the neck. This enlargement and a positive test for antibodies are signs of active disease. The patient may transmit the virus by sexual contact and blood transfer. In addition, some patients in this stage are troubled by symptoms that include fever, night sweats, fatigue, diarrhea, and weight loss. People with these symptoms should be evaluated by a physician to determine if one of the opportunistic diseases found in Stage IV has developed.

Specific questions may arise when a child or adult with a Stage II or Stage III condition needs or wants a vaccination—particularly with a live virus such as the smallpox or polio virus. To introduce a second virus into the system could theoretically tip the balance of the immune system to the advantage of any of these viruses present. To be sure of what is best, individuals in this situation should consult with a physician.

STAGE IV: BURNOUT (THE ACTUAL ACQUIRED IMMUNE DEFICIENCY SYNDROME)

With the passage of time, AIDS has developed in an increasing number of people who were initially in Stages II or III. The burnout stage of the HIV infection corresponds to the initially described Acquired Immune Deficiency Syndrome (AIDS). The clinical diagnosis of AIDS is not based on laboratory tests but on a typical clinical picture that is the result of the HIV disease having exhausted most of, or all, of the host cells (so-called T-cells of the immune system) in the body. The body no longer has a defense against other infections, and because some cancers are controlled by the immune system, no defense against these either.

The infections and tumors that appear are called "opportunistic invaders." They are uncommon medical problems except in very debilitated or old people or in people who are purposely deprived of their normal immune system, such as the recipients of organ transplants. When the immune system is broken down by the HIV virus, these diseases take the opportunity to invade any accessible part of the body.

AIDS is observed after an average of about three to five years of slow HIV infection, but may develop as early as seven months or as late as seven years after the start of Stage II or III. What occurs after seven years is not known yet because the HIV disease has not been known that long. A person with AIDS will usually be quite ill from all the complications of having an impaired immune system.

The clinical picture of AIDS depends on which opportunistic disease becomes evident first. The most common diseases seen as part of AIDS are:

1. PNEUMOCYSTIS CARINII, a small protozoan parasite which causes pneumonia.

2. CYTOMEGALOVIRUS (CMV), a virus of the herpes family which tends to go rampant when the immune system fails.

3. CANDIDIASIS, a fungal infection which may cause infection in the mouth, esophagus, and lungs and seriously interferes with eating or breathing.

4. CRYPTOSPORIDIOSIS, a parasite that tends to invade the intestine and cause a very debilitation diarrhea.

5. TOXOPLASMA GONDII, a parasite which might cause abscesses in the brain.

6. CRYPTOCOCCUS, a fungus which infects and spreads all through the body, causing a generalized feeling of malaise, weakness, and may also cause meningitis.

7. KAPOSI'S SARCOMA, a very unusual skin cancer, which, when occurring in non-AIDS patients, usually affects elderly people. The tumor is malignant and appears first in the skin. In AIDS patients, it may affect the skin anywhere in the body. Eventually, the tumor will spread internally throughout the body. The condition may become debilitating and will often be followed by the onset of one of the above-listed opportunistic infections.

When any of the opportunistic infections or tumors break out in a defenseless AIDS patient, the infection becomes very difficult to control. Patients go in and out of the hospital, most of the time remaining under medical care. After an average of one year, the AIDS patient will die from one of the conditions listed above.

THE SPREAD OF HIV-DISEASE

It has been postulated that the HIV infection may have entered the human race somewhere in Central Africa. Here the virus is equally common among males and females. In the rest of the world it has remained a disease predominantly affecting homosexual males and intravenous drug users. Still, as of today, 17 percent of the cases in the United States appear in heterosexuals. Although the virus has been shown to be present in saliva and tears, transmission of the virus via these body fluids has not occurred. On the basis of this evidence, we can conclude that the HIV virus is spread by sexual fluids or by infected blood. Transmission of the virus by casual contacts in environments such as schools, work, or other public places has not occurred.

The geographic spread of AIDS in the U.S. is remarkable in that 84 percent of the cases have been reported from only five states: New York, California, Florida, New Jersey, and Texas. Over 64 percent of the cases have been reported from the metropolitan areas of New York City, San Francisco, Los Angeles, and Miami. Most other reports also come from metropolitan areas of larger cities. The average age for males with AIDS is only 35 years.

The patterns of incidence of AIDS in the population tells much about how the HIV disease is spread. Outside the homosexual community, HIV disease has affected people who have been in contact with infected blood either from blood transfusions or by unclean, blood-contaminated needles such as those used by drug abusers. The spread of the disease in Western countries has taken place sometime between the late 1970s and the present. The spread of AIDS by blood transfusions or blood products has been controlled since late 1984, when blood banks learned how to screen out infected blood by checking it for HIV antibodies.

One further word about blood transfusions is appropriate. Laboratory tests can detect the presence of HIV antibodies, an indication that the person has been exposed to the HIV virus. This test has made the blood supply safe for transfusion recipients. Blood donors were never at risk of contracting the HIV virus. Obviously, people who are not fully well, for any reason, should refrain from giving blood.

Newborn children of mothers infected with the HIV virus may themselves become infected. The actual mode of transmission from mother to child is thought to occur in the womb. Newborn children normally have a less developed immune system than adults and may therefore be at higher risk for AIDS. Older children exposed only to casual contact with HIV-infected persons are not at any risk to contract the disease. Similarly, in families where a child has AIDS, there has not been a transmission of the HIV virus between children and adults living in the same household.

Because the HIV virus is spread only by contact with contaminated blood, sexual fluids, and maternal transmission, it is possible to control or contain its spread. Precautions have to be the same as for other venereal diseases such as gonorrhea or syphilis; know your own health and that of your sexual partner. Limit sexual contacts to exclusive relationships or use condoms for protection.

As of 1987, there is no truly effective cure for AIDS and the prospects for the near future are not encouraging. Many scientists are pursuing avenues that will lead to a vaccine or to a cure. But, until then, the best hope is prevention, a responsibility that each of us has—to protect our own good health.

Through trial and error, doctors have developed a "cocktail" of medicines to enhance the antibody system of the AIDS patient in order to keep the HIV-virus growth in neutral balance and also to control the outbreak of the opportunistic diseases. Thanks to this technique, deaths from AIDS in the United States have decreased 70 percent from 51,670 in 1995 to 15,603 in 2001.

A DESCRIPTION AND SCHEMATIC
OF THE HIV DISEASE

The HIV infection has four clinical stages:

Stage I

INVASION

Flu-like symptoms, fever, weakness, and muscle ache often lead to:

GROWTH

Swollen lymph nodes in neck, armpit, groin—weight loss, weakness, fevers, night sweats, diarrhea lasting several days or weeks. Stage I leads to one of the two balanced stages:

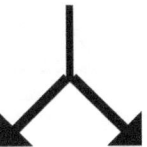

Stage III
ARC

Laboratory sign plus enlarged lymph nodes otherwise feeling well

Stage II
ASYMPTOMATIC

Only laboratory signs of the disease; feeling well

Stage IV
BURNOUT
(AIDS SYNDROME)

Patient has opportunistic infections or tumors

Immune System in a Healthy Person

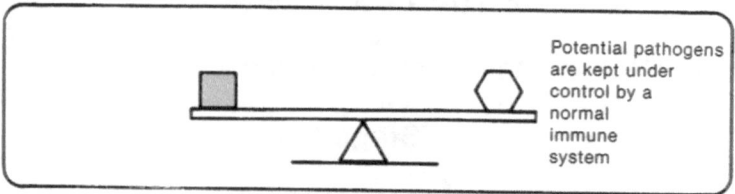

Immune System in a Person with HIV Disease

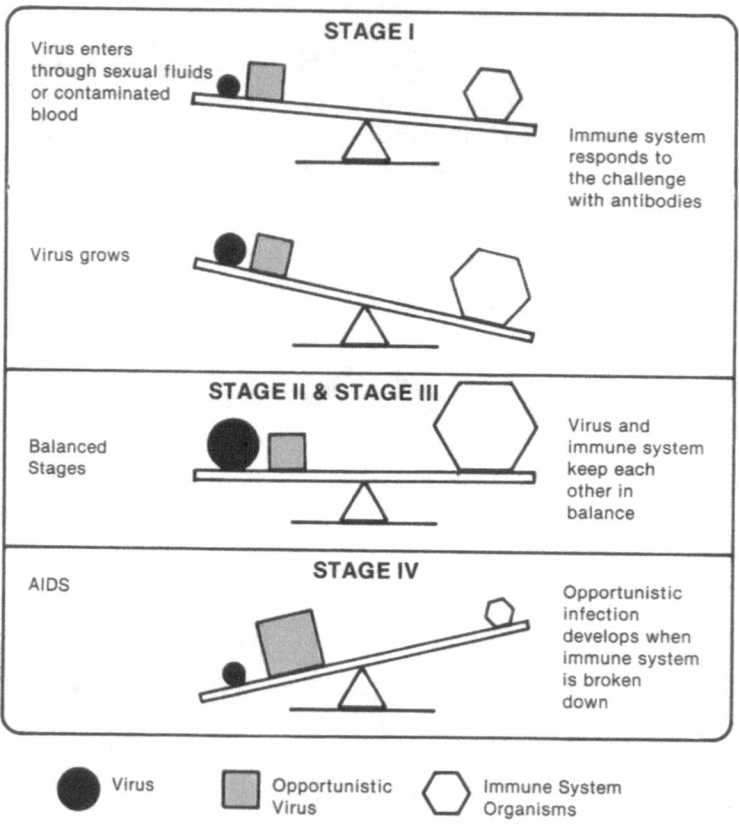

HIV/AIDS STATISTICS

HIV/AIDS WORLDWIDE

- As of the end of 2002, an estimated 42 million people worldwide (38.6 million adults and 3.2 million children younger than 15 years) were living with HIV/AIDS. Approximately 70 percent of these people (29.4 million) live in Sub-Saharan Africa; another 17 percent (7.2 million) live in Asia.(1)

- Worldwide, approximately 12 of every 1000 adults aged 15 to 49 are HIV-infected. In Sub-Saharan Africa, about 9 percent of all adults in this age group are HIV-infected. In four African countries, the prevalence of HIV infection among adults aged 15 to 49 exceeds 30 percent.(1)

- Approximately 50 percent of adults living with HIV/AIDS worldwide are women.(1)

- An estimated 5 million new HIV infections occurred worldwide during 2002; that is, about 14,000 infections each day. More than 95 percent of these new infections occurred in developing countries.(1)

- In 2002, approximately 2,000 children under the age of 15 years, and 6,000 young people aged 15 to 24 years became infected with HIV every day.(1)

- In 2002 alone, HIV/AIDS-associated illnesses caused the deaths of approximately 3.1 million people worldwide, including an estimated 610,000 children younger than 15 years.(1)

HIV/AIDS IN THE UNITED STATES

- The Centers for Disease Control and Prevention (CDC) estimate that 850,000 to 950,000 U.S. residents are living with HIV infection, one-quarter of whom are unaware of their infection.[2]

- Approximately 40,000 new HIV infections occur each

year in the United States, about 70 percent among men and 30 percent among women. **Of these newly infected people, half are younger than 25 years of age.** [3,4]

- Of newly infected men, approximately 50 percent are black, 30 percent are white, 20 percent are Hispanic, and a small percentage are members of other racial/ ethnic groups. [4]

- Of new infections among women in the United States, CDC estimates that approximately 75 percent of women were infected through heterosexual sex and 25 percent through injection drug use. Of newly infected women, approximately 64 percent are black, 18 percent are white, 18 percent are Hispanic, and a small percentage are members of other racial/ethnic groups. [4]

- In the United States, 816,149 cases of AIDS had been reported to the CDC through December 2001. [5]

- The estimated number of new adult/ adolescent AIDS cases diagnosed in the United States was 60,805 in 1996, 49,646 in 1997, 42,832 in 1998, 41,165 in 1999, 40,766 in 2000, and 41,311 in 2001. [5]

- The estimated number of new pediatric (individuals younger than age 13) AIDS cases in the United States fell from 954 in 1992 to 101 in 2001. [5]

- The rate of adult/adolescent AIDS cases reported in the United States in 2001 (per 100,000 population) was 76.3 among blacks, 28.0 among Hispanics, 11.7 among American Indians/Alaska Natives, 7.9 among whites, and 4.8 among Asians/Pacific Islanders. [5]

- From 1985 to 2001, the proportion of adult/adolescent AIDS cases in the United States reported in women increased from 7 to 25 percent. [5]

- As of the end of 2001, an estimated 362,827 people in the United States were living with AIDS. [5]

- As of December 31, 2001, 467,910 deaths among people with AIDS had been reported to the CDC. [5] AIDS is now the fifth leading cause of death in the United States among people aged 25 to 44, and is the leading cause of death for black men in this age group.[6]

- The estimated annual number of AIDS-related deaths in the United States fell approximately 70 percent from 1995 to 2001, from 51,670 deaths in 1995 to 15,603 deaths in 2001.[5]

- Of the estimated 15,603 AIDS-related deaths in the United States in 2001, approximately 52 percent were among blacks, 29 percent among whites, 18 percent among Hispanics, and less than 1 percent among Asians/Pacific Islanders and American Indians/Alaska Natives.[5]

REFERENCES

1.   UNAIDS. AIDS Epidemic Update. December. 2002.

2.   Fleming, P.L. et al. HIV Prevalence in the United States. 2000. 9th Conference on Retroviruses and Opportunistic Infections, Seattle, Wash., Feb. 24-28, 2002. Abstract 11.

3.   Centers for Disease Control and Prevention (CDC). HIV and AIDS - United States. 1981-2001. MMWR 2001; 50:430-434.

4.   Centers for Disease Control and Prevention (CDC). HIV Prevention Strategic Plan through 2005. January 2001.

5.   Centers for Disease Control and Prevention (CDC). HIV/AIDS Surveillance Report 2001; 13 (No. 2):1-44.

6.   Deaths: Final Data for 2000. National Vital Statistics Reports; Vol. 50, No. 15. Hyattsville, Maryland: National Center for Health Statistics, 2002.

Gunnar G. Sevelius, M.D.

RECOMMENDATIONS

Transmission of the HIV virus occurs only by sexual and blood fluids. Therefore:

1. The HIV infection is preventable.
2. Know the health of your sexual partner and/or use a condom.
3. Take precautions for loved ones if you have a positive blood test.
4. Many places offer free anonymous blood tests. Call the AIDS Hotline in your area.

SUMMARY

The HIV infection has officially been declared the most urgent health problem in the U.S.

The HIV infection is caused by a virus which is currently transmitted by sexual fluids, contaminated blood and maternal transmission.

The HIV infection has never been documented to be transmitted by casual contact.

There is no cure for HIV. For now, prevention is the best hope. This is your responsibility.

DENTAL HEALTH

or

How to Keep Your Smile

J. W. Goodhart, R.D.H.

Foreword by

Dr. Samuel Wycoff, D.M.D., M.P.H.

*Every tooth in a man's head
is more valuable than a diamond.*

Miguel de Cervantes (1547-1616)

From Don Quixote

FOREWORD

Approximately one-fifth of most large corporations' medical bills are allocated to dental health care. Ninety-nine percent of dental disease is preventable with proper home care. Therefore, the primary goal of the dental profession should be, and has been education and preventive measures.

This effort has contributed to the recent reduction in the prevalence of dental decay among children and young adults in the United States. This reduction has been marked and dramatic and is likely to continue. The reduction has been achieved largely through fluoridation of public water supplies and other uses of fluoride. Such preventive successes have been boosted by significant improvements in treatment technology as well as increased scientific understanding of the causes of the most prevalent oral diseases—caries and periodontal diseases.

While dental decay has declined due to effective preventive measures, little attention has been focused on the trends in the periodontal diseases (gum diseases), which have long been considered to be the major adult oral disease and the principal reason for loss of teeth in persons over age 35. Therefore, increased attention must be paid to the prevention of periodontal disease in addition to continuing the prevention of cavities.

Major opportunities for reducing health care costs while improving the public's health can be found in what people do, or do not do, to and for themselves. Educating people about their ability and responsibility to protect and maintain their own health is a primary objective of this Dental Health chapter.

Samuel Wycoff

INTRODUCTION

Even though most of us are aware that we must care for our teeth, many of us do not do enough before it is too late. For normally healthy people, problems with teeth do not show up before a lot of damage has already occurred.

In this chapter you will find a brief history of tooth problems, a description of oral anatomy, as well as a discussion of the causes, symptoms, and con-sequences of dental disease. In addition, remedies and prevention will be described. Most people lose their teeth as a result of neglect. When dental disease has progressed to the point of no return, the remedies may be limited to removal of teeth, which is painful and costly. Even just a few extra minutes a day can make the difference between a healthy set of teeth and losing some or all of them. Prevention is still the best remedy.

HISTORY

As long as people have existed, we have suffered from dental problems. Our earliest fossil finds of the human species show evidence of tooth decay, gum disease, and wear. Although these early peoples' life expectancy was around 30, most were even younger when they died. They didn't have the time to develop the long-term problems that we experience today. As life expectancy increased, tooth problems increased accordingly.

All civilizations have had tooth remedies in their medical practices. Herbal cures for toothaches were commonly used. Socrates recommended cleaning tartar off of the teeth to cure infected gums. The earliest toothbrushes were sticks chewed on the ends, then used to clean the teeth (some cultures still use these). None of them worked, however, and people usually lost their teeth.

**George Washington owned at least
six sets of artificial teeth**

Crude dentures have been made from wood, animal teeth, bone, pewter and other materials that could be fashioned to look like teeth. We all know about George Washington's dentures, which were so uncomfortable that he only wore them on ceremonial occasions. Very primitive people simply died when they could no longer chew their food. It is no wonder then, that saving teeth has been a high priority to us for as long as we have been aware that we could save them.

Near the end of the 19th century, a dentist discovered that nitrous oxide (laughing gas) prevented pain during surgery. Before then, doctors had their patients become as drunk as possible before any operation. Being able to work on people without causing pain enabled dentists (and doctors) to develop new methods for saving teeth that, until then, would have been removed. Today, the modern science of dentistry can do what these early pioneers would have called miracles.

ORAL ANATOMY

To understand dental problems, and what is done about them, we must first be able to recognize the structures of the mouth.

To begin with, the mouth is composed of the lips, cheeks, tongue, roof (palate), floor, teeth and gums. Some would also include the entrance to the throat, uvula and tonsils. Our emphasis will be mainly on the teeth and gums.

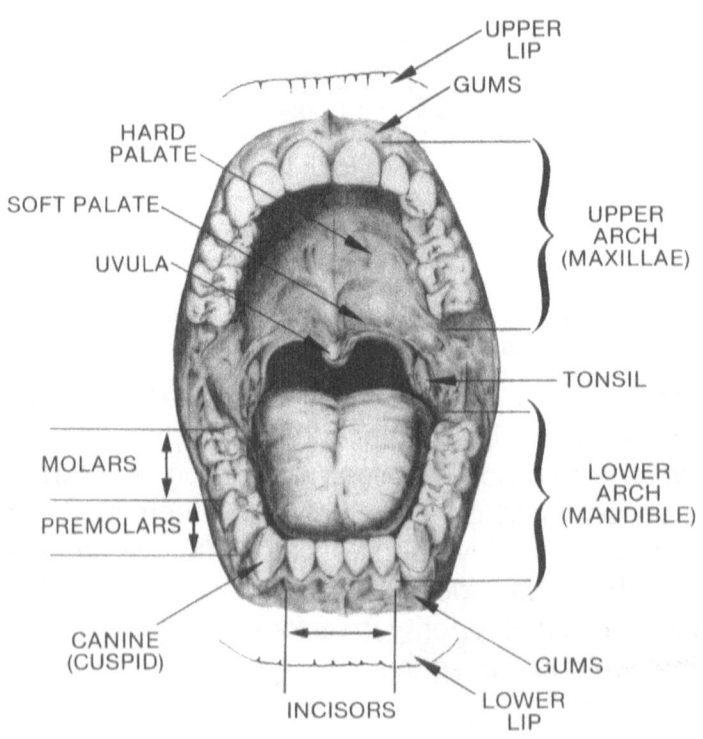

Each tooth consists of a root (that part which is embedded in the socket of the jaw) and a crown (that part above the gums). If you take a tooth out and look at it, the root looks different from the crown, because the crown is covered with enamel, while the root is covered by a much softer substance called *cementum.* Enamel is very hard (about as hard as surgical steel) and smooth, which is why it is able to resist 70 or 80 years of wear. Cementum is about as hard as bone and is ideal for the fibers that attach the tooth to the socket.

Looking at a cross-section of the tooth, you will notice that under both the enamel and cementum is a material called *dentin.* Dentin makes up the bulk of the hard structure of the tooth and is composed of thousands of hollow tubules that lead from the surface of the tooth inward to the center. The center is filled with blood vessels, nerves and tissue and is called the *pulp* (most people call this the nerve). This is the heart of the tooth. Blood vessels enter the tooth through an opening in the root tip called the *apical foramen.* The cells that line the pulp, where it meets the dentin, are stimulated when the tooth is damaged, and lay down new dentin to protect the tooth from further damage. This is why teeth will sometimes become sensitive for a while then the sensitivity gradually goes away.

Surrounding the tooth is what dentists call the *periodontium* *(perio*, around; *dontium-*, tooth). This is made up of the gums, the socket, and the lining of the socket. The socket that the tooth sits in is in either the upper or lower jaws (*maxillae* or *mandible*), and is made up of the bone of that jaw. The socket is lined with the peridontal ligament, which is a system of little fibers that attach to the tooth and the bone of the socket, holding the tooth firmly in place while allowing enough movement to absorb the pressures our jaw muscles put on them. The gums are connective tissue that surround and protect the base of the teeth and the bone.

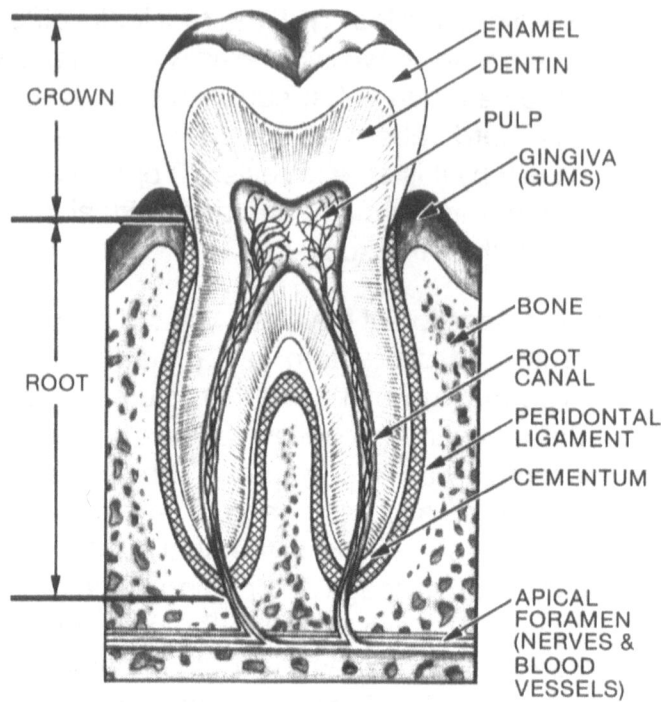

Cross-section of a Healthy Tooth

These structures will be discussed in more detail in our discussion of dental problems.

TIMING OF CHILDREN'S TEETH

When are my child's teeth supposed to come in? Is it normal to get them at any particular age? These are commonly asked questions in any dental office. The answers are as individual as each child. Some babies are born with their front teeth already present, others don't develop them for many months. Each child has its own rate of development. But there are some averages that dentists use as guidelines.

The following chart will show when the baby teeth come in, are lost, and the permanent teeth replace them. Generally the lower teeth come in before the upper teeth. Remember, these are average numbers and your child will not necessarily get their teeth at these times.

Two things need to be mentioned: First, the baby teeth keep the spaces open for the permanent teeth to come into. These should be cared for just as if they were permanent teeth. Second, the six-year molars that come in behind the child's baby molars are permanent teeth. People commonly think that because these teeth don't replace any baby teeth, that they are also baby teeth, and will eventually be lost. Not true! Please protect these teeth as you would any object to be kept for 80 years.

If your child seems to vary from these general patterns by more than a few months, see your dentist. Hopefully, children are seeing their dentist every six months, in which case he/she is probably watching the child's development as closely (or closer) than you are. Many parents, however, do not bring their children to the dentist until they are 3 or 4 years old, or older. The parent, therefore, needs to be aware if there is some unusual teething pattern that should be brought to the attention of their dentist.

	AVERAGE AGE TEETH ERUPT	AVERAGE AGE TEETH ARE SHED
UPPER		
Central incisor ...	8–12 mo.	6–7 yr.
Lateral incisor ...	9–13 mo.	7–8 yr.
Canine	16–22 mo.	0–12 yr.
First molar	13–19 mo.	9–11 yr.
Second molar	25–33 mo.	0–12 yr.
LOWER		
Second molar	23–31 mo.	0–12 yr.
First molar	14–18 mo.	9–11 yr.
Canine	17–23 mo.	9–12 yr.
Lateral incisor ..	10–16 mo.	7–8 yr.
Central incisor ..	6–10 mo.	6–7 yr.

LEFT   RIGHT

PRIMARY
BABY
TEETH

UPPER	
Central incisor	7–8 yr.
Lateral incisor	8–9 yr.
Canine	11–12 yr.
First premolar	10–11 yr.
Second premolar ...	10–12 yr.
First molar	6–7 yr.
Second molar	12–13 yr.
Third molar	17–21 yr.
LOWER	
Third molar	17–21 yr.
Second molar	11–13 yr.
First molar	6–7 yr.
Second premolar ...	11–12 yr.
First premolar	10–12 yr.
Canine	9–10 yr.
Lateral incisor	7–8 yr.
Central incisor	6–7 yr.

PERMANENT
TEETH

LEFT   RIGHT

Tooth Eruption Patterns and Identification

There are ten primary teeth that are generally identified by letters A through T. Permanent teeth are identified by numbers 1 through 32. Premolars are generally referred to as "bicuspids" and third molars are generally referred to as "wisdom teeth." See chart.

THE CAUSES OF DENTAL DISEASE

Most dental disease is caused by *plaque,* a film of bacteria that builds up on your teeth every day. It comes from the bacteria that are naturally present in your mouth. They aid in digestion and form a protective barrier to disease-causing bacteria and funguses. But when they combine to form the groups of bacteria that cause cavities and gum disease, they are harmful. To do this, they must be organized in a certain way and there must be enough of them (they must be a certain thickness). This process takes only 24 hours. Plaque can destroy the bone that holds your teeth in. Avoidance of these problems will be discussed in the prevention section of this pamphlet.

Cavities start with plaque building up on the teeth and being left there. The plaque attacks the teeth by putting out very acidic waste products which chemically eat away the tooth. The acids that the bacteria produce slowly begin to destroy the enamel of the crown. Enamel is very hard and resists this attack for a long time, but in the grooves on the chewing surfaces of the back teeth and at the gum line, where the crown and the root meet, enamel is thinner and harder to clean. These are usually the places where decay will start first. Another hard to clean area is in between the teeth. After the enamel has been destroyed, the plaque can enter the soft dentin under it. Once this happens, the decay goes much faster. The bacteria can go through the tubules in the dentin to the pulp, which reacts to this invasion by laying down more reparative dentin. If the decay is removed and the tooth filled at this point, the process stops and the tooth is restored to normal (dentists call fillings, restorations). If it is neglected, the area of decay grows rapidly, and the pulp becomes more infected. Eventually, the pulp will become so damaged that it will die and an abscess will form. By this time, one will usually have a toothache and have to go to the dentist.

Many people have a great many cavities, resulting in many fillings and crowns. These people often think they have "soft" teeth. Most dentists agree that there is no such thing as soft teeth, but rather teeth that decay readily. Things such as high fever in early childhood can interfere with enamel development in permanent teeth. This causes the teeth to be more easily decayed, but not what a dentist would call soft.

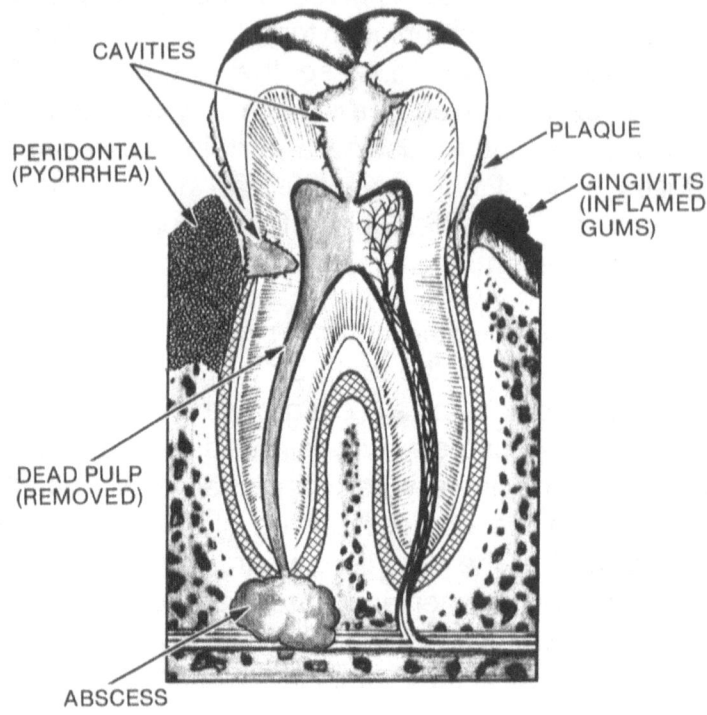

Cross-section of a Tooth Showing Dental Disease

Another very serious problem that we all suffer from is gum disease (periodontal disease, or *pyorrhea).* This is the cause of most tooth loss after age 40. Plaque also causes this disease by building up, mainly between the teeth, and being left there. The same waste products that cause decay, cause the gum tissue to become irritated and inflamed. The early stage of this process is called *gingivitis* (inflamed gums). The gums become puffy and red, and may bleed easily. With the gums continually infected, the bone of the socket of the tooth is gradually destroyed, and can no longer support the teeth. Teeth become loose, gums hurt, and bad breath will result. People are usually willing to do anything to save their teeth, including costly surgery, but it is often too late. Their teeth have to go and be replaced by dentures.

FILLINGS, CROWNS, BRIDGES AND DENTURES

Fillings. A filling is either metal or plastic that is placed in a very precisely prepared area of a tooth to restore it to normal function. This means that after decay (or sometimes a fracture) causes the tooth to be partially destroyed, the dentist cuts into the tooth with a high-speed drill (up to 500,000 rpm), removes the decay, creates a shape that will hold the filling, places the filling material, then carves it back to the normal shape of the tooth. The tooth has been "restored" to normal function.

To fill back teeth, silver alloy and gold are used (these are not usually used in the front of the mouth for esthetic reasons). Silver alloy is the most common because it is easy to use, very strong and durable, and relatively inexpensive. It can last an entire lifetime, or only a few years.

Gold is also used as a filling material. This is usually accomplished by the dentist preparing the tooth, taking an impression of the tooth, sending the impression to a lab which makes the filling, putting a temporary filling in the tooth, and finally cementing in the gold filling. It is easy to see why these fillings cost four or five times as much as silver.

To fill cavities in the front of the mouth where they can be seen, one of several plastic filling materials is used. All are much better than they were five years ago. If decay is present in the tooth, the dentist prepares it much the same as the back teeth. The plastic material is then placed in the preparation, shaped properly, and allowed to "set" hard (by using a special light). The filling is then shaped to the tooth so that the edges are undetectable.

Using a new technique called bonding, the new plastic materials can be applied to a tooth using a mild acid to "etch" the enamel.

The acid erodes the enamel just enough to cause it to be rough. The plastic is then placed on the tooth and will adhere to this rough surface and stay in place. This is a very useful procedure that has enabled dentists to cover badly stained or discolored teeth without capping them. Although some people want to use bonding to have whiter teeth, there are several problems: first, the filling material will sometimes start to chip off after four or five years and must be replaced; second, when used to cover all of the teeth, they will look bulky and unnatural; third, insurance companies consider bonding for esthetics (looks) only and refuse to pay for them.

Crowns. Fillings eventually break down and must be replaced. Each time this is done, a little more of the tooth is lost. Eventually, there is not enough tooth material left to hold a filling in. If decay is allowed to go too long, too much of the tooth may be lost to permit a filling. As a final resort, to maintain the integrity of the tooth, the dentist may crown it.

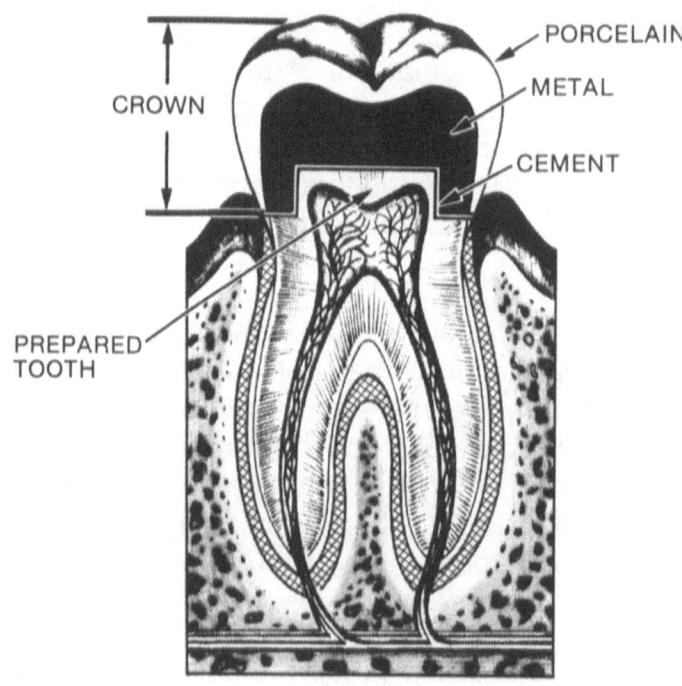

Porcelain Fused to Metal Crown

The dentist trims the tooth down into a very precise shape, much like a peg. An impression of the tooth is sent to a dental lab where the crown is handmade to fit exactly over the tooth in the exact shape of the tooth as it was before. The bulk of the crown is made of either gold alloy or other semiprecious metal. This is done so that it will have the strength to resist the forces exerted by the jaws (up to 10,000 pounds per square inch). If the crown will be located where it can be seen in the patient's mouth, i. e., in the smile line, a porcelain cover is hand painted on the metal, and then baked at an extremely high temperature. When all of this is finished, the patient comes back to have the crown cemented into place. The bite is checked to make sure that the crown meets the other teeth properly. If the crown feels too high, it should be corrected immediately.

Crowns are costly because of the large amount of professional time and materials involved. Having teeth "capped" for appearance only is not covered by dental insurance.

Bridges. If a tooth is lost for some reason, and is not replaced soon thereafter, the teeth on either side of the space will tend to lean into it, and the tooth above or below may start to grow into the space (teeth grow until they meet another tooth). To prevent this from happening, a bridge can be constructed if there is a tooth on either side of the space.

A bridge is like three or more crowns that are made as one piece. The office procedure for making the bridge is the same as for a single crown described above. The teeth on either side of the space are prepared for crowns; impressions are taken, and then sent to the lab where the three (or more) crowns are cast as one piece of metal. If they will be visible, they are porcelain covered to match the color of the other teeth. The dentist then cements the crowns onto the teeth on either side of the space, just as with a single crown. The crown or crowns in the middle then replace the missing tooth or teeth. This is called a permanent fixed replacement, because it may never have to be redone. Dentists expect to get at least five years of wear from a bridge; most last much longer.

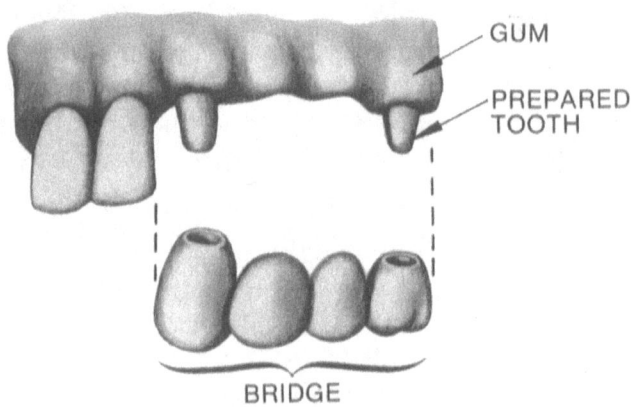

GUM

PREPARED TOOTH

BRIDGE

A Permanent Bridge

If there is no tooth behind the missing tooth, or if cost is a factor, a removable partial denture can be made. These have clasps that hold onto the adjacent tooth, and a plate covering the palate, if it is for upper teeth, or a bar under the tongue around the lower arch. A partial denture can be taken out for cleaning. Partials are good replacements if a bridge cannot be made, although most people have trouble getting used to them. They should be taken out at night to let the tissues under them rest, but should not be left out too long as the teeth in the mouth will move, causing the denture not to fit when it is put back in.

Dentures. There are two kinds of dentures: those that replace some missing teeth, called partial dentures, and those that replace all of the teeth, called complete dentures. We have previously discussed partial dentures.

Complete dentures, or false teeth, replace all of the teeth of the upper or lower arch or both. This is the last resort in dentistry. A complete upper plate can be quite comfortable and secure due to the suction between the *palate* (roof of the mouth) and the denture, which usually covers the entire palate. Complete lower dentures are very difficult to keep in place because they only have the bony ridge of the lower arch to adhere to. After dentures have been worn for several years, the ridge becomes increasingly flattened, leading to decreased adherence. To keep complete dentures fitting as well as they can, they must be relined periodically; a new set often has to be made every 6 to 10 years (sometimes more often).

Implants. Implants are stainless steel bars that are implanted into the lower arch to hold a lower denture in place. To make one, the gum tissue is opened surgically and an impression is taken of the bone. Then a stainless steel device is made that sits on the bone, with a bar protruding through the gums into the mouth. The gums are sutured together over the steel and allowed to heal. A new lower denture is then made that clamps onto the steel bar. Although implants are quite good for holding the denture securely, often the implant is rejected. Coupled with the very high cost of this procedure, we must think long and hard about whether it is worthwhile.

DENTAL SURGERY

Root Canals. A root canal is a name for a procedure that is done when the pulp of the tooth is dead due to disease or trauma. This may occur when decay is allowed to go too long untreated, often leading to an abscess being formed at the tip of the root. Your dentist may also judge that the trauma of a particularly extensive dental procedure, may cause the pulp to die with possible risk for an abscess at a later date. In both of these cases a root canal procedure must be done.

To do a root canal, the dentist opens a hole into the pulp (nerve) of the tooth. Then a series of small files and reamers are used to clean out and smooth down the area where the pulp was. This is then sterilized to kill any remaining bacteria. If the tooth is abscessed, a medicated filling will be used to treat the tooth before final filling. Antibiotics may be prescribed to make sure the infection is gone. The canals are then filled using a root canal sealer. If necessary, a permanent filling, or a crown, using a small gold post is inserted into one of the canals so the tooth will not become brittle and break. A filled canal results in a tooth nearly as good as a normal one. It can last just as long, and be just as comfortable as any other tooth.

Wisdom Teeth. Wisdom teeth got their name because they come in when we are much older, and, hopefully, "wiser". Most of us do not have enough room in our mouth for them. They often come in at strange angles or only partially. Even those of us who have enough room for our wisdom teeth to come in straight often have trouble keeping them clean. They decay quickly and we have to invest a lot of money to save them. Most wisdom teeth eventually have to be removed.

Wisdom teeth (called third molars) are no more difficult to remove than any other tooth, and upper wisdom teeth are the easiest teeth of them all to remove, according to many dentists. Those of us who have trouble with these teeth must have them extracted. Even the most difficult wisdom teeth can be removed easily by a good oral surgeon.

BRACES

There are many good reasons for having our bites corrected with braces. Lack of space is the most frequent cause for correction. The arches (upper and lower row of teeth) of our mouth are formed by our skull. If our teeth take up more room than our arches provide, there is only one way for them to go and that is to twist and jumble around so that they fit into the space available. Everyone is familiar with what crowded teeth look like. Other conditions such as teeth not meeting correctly, overbites, underbites, crossbites, all require correction by an orthodontist, the specialist who handles straightening of teeth.

Teeth are moved by putting force on them for a period of time. Certain cells in the lining of the tooth socket eat bone and others build bone. The pressure applied by the braces causes the cells on the side of the tooth away from the pressure to destroy some of the bone on that side. On the other side (the side to which pressure is applied) the bone building cells go to work. The bone is gradually dissolved on the side away from the pressure and built on the other side so that the tooth slowly moves in the intended direction. If too much pressure is applied, the root of the tooth instead of the socket may be attacked by the cells, resulting in very short, rounded roots that may not last into adulthood. For this reason, braces usually require at least a year and a half to two years (less time for minor corrections, more for major).

Some conditions must be corrected surgically. The lower or upper jaw may need to be shortened or lengthened. This is done in a hospital operating room under general anesthesia. The teeth must be wired together for 2 to 8 weeks after the operation to allow the bones to heal. Braces are used afterward to place the teeth in balance and the person is better than new.

A final word on braces. A person is almost never too old to have them as long as there is good bone support around the teeth. The oldest people in braces are in their 70s. If you have a bite problem and you are no longer a teenager, you can still have it corrected. Many orthodontists report up to half of their patients are adults.

PREVENTION

There are several ways to prevent dental disease: fluoride, brushing, flossing, cleaning and regular checkups with x-rays. Diet also plays a part in prevention.

FLUORIDE

Fluoride is the sixteenth most abundant element in nature. A medical researcher stumbled over its ability to prevent cavities while trying to discover the cause of another illness in a community. The people of the community had brown stained teeth but no cavities. It was suspected that fluoride in the drinking water was the cause. In 1945 drinking water supplies for some large cities were fluoridated at one part per million (ppm). Some naturally fluoridated water contains as much as 35-40 ppm, such as in the one where the researcher first noticed its effects. Since then, many cities have added fluoride to their water, with the result that children in these places grow up with very few cavities.

If the city you live in does not have the optimal level fluoride in its water, start your children at birth on fluoride drops or tablets. Your dentist or pediatrician can prescribe them for you. If the fluoride is taken until about age 12, it will be absorbed by the teeth while they are forming.

Children should also be taken to the dentist every six months for fluoride treatments. This is the next most effective type of treatment. Schools are offering fluoride rinse programs. While not as effective as office treatments, these are also very good. Toothpaste containing fluoride should also be used. This is the least effective type of treatment, and alone will not prevent as many cavities. Used along with the other fluorides mentioned, the result will be far less decay for your children.

Along with fluoride, brushing and flossing are effective methods of preventing decay and gum disease. They work by disturbing the plaque. As you will recall, plaque needs to be a certain thickness, and it must be organized before it can cause disease. If we floss at least once a day, and brush twice, we can keep the thickness down and the rest disorganized. If we do this consistently for the rest of our lives, we should all have our teeth for as long as we live and should have a minimum of decay and gum problems. We must use both floss and brush, because one cleans where the other will not.

BRUSHING

Everyone knows they should brush their teeth, but not everyone knows the right way. To begin with, most authorities recommend using a soft-bristled brush. Remember, plaque is a sticky film like wet paint on a window.

Place the bristles at a 45-degree angle to the tooth at the gum line. Then using a vibrating motion, or a small circular motion, clean the gum line area. Plaque hides in the crevice between the tooth and gum. This motion forces the bristles up into the crevice so that they can sweep away the plaque. When this is finished, sweep the brush down on the top teeth, or up on the lower teeth. This cleans the crown of the tooth. Then move the brush forward or back in the mouth half a brush length, and repeat the procedure. Do this on the inside and the outside of all your teeth. The size of the arch is usually too narrow on the tongue side of the lower front teeth to use the width of the brush, so turn the brush lengthwise to clean this area (see diagram).

If you have any difficulties with brushing or flossing, see your dentist or hygienist and they will be happy to help you.

A word of caution. Do not use a scrubbing (long back and forth) motion to brush your teeth. This is a very natural motion for most people to use. The problem is that over a period of years, you can wear a groove at the gum line of the tooth that can become sensitive and need to be filled. In extreme cases, the teeth can die from the trauma and need root canals. Using the method of brushing described above will do a beautiful job of cleaning your teeth with no damage to them.

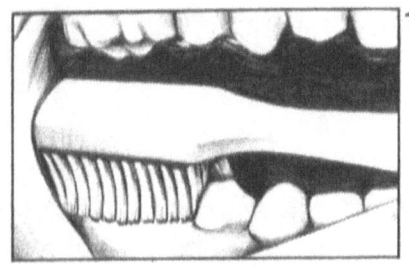

1. Position the toothbrush at roughly a 45° angle to the gum line.

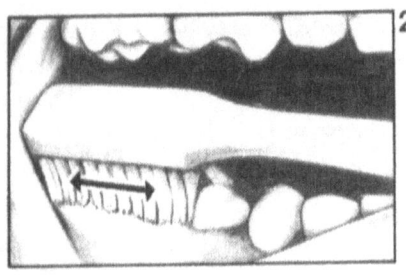

2. Vibrate back and fourth with short strokes.

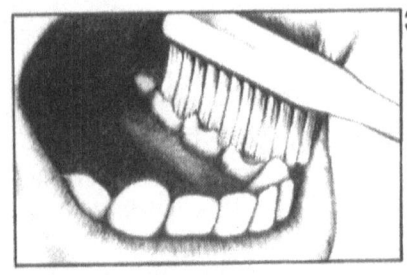

3. Brush outer, inner and biting surfaces of each tooth.

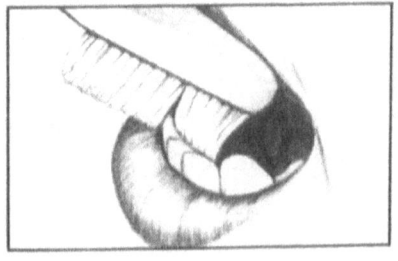

4. Use toe of brush for inside of front teeth.

Brushing

FLOSSING

Flossing is probably the single most important thing you can do for your teeth. If done daily, up to 90 percent of dental disease can be prevented. Find a time during your busy day when it is convenient to spend five minutes flossing, and try to make a habit of doing it every day at this time. Right before brushing is a very good time for many people.

Begin by pulling off 12 to 24 inches of floss. Wrap both ends around your middle fingers. Wrap more around one hand than the other so that as you use it, you can unwind it from that hand and wind it around the other. Then holding the floss with the index fingers about one inch apart, gently saw the floss back and forth between the teeth. Don't snap it down between them as this can damage the tissue, even cut it, causing soreness and bleeding. When the floss is between the teeth, push with both fingers toward the back tooth so that the floss wraps against it, then, using pressure, rub the floss up and down cleaning the entire side of the tooth. You will need to do this three or four times to remove the plaque. Remember, you are trying to remove a sticky film of bacteria, something like removing wet paint from a window, so spend a little time at it. After that surface is clean, lift the floss up over the gum and pull against the tooth in front. Rub up and down a few times, then seesaw the floss back out from between the teeth and move on to the next spot. Repeat this until every tooth has been cleaned on both sides.

It is a good idea to go around your mouth in the same pattern each time you floss. For example, start on the lower right back molars and work around to the back left. Then move up to the upper left and work around to the right. It doesn't matter where you start and stop as long as you do it the same each time. This is important because you are less likely to miss when you use the same pattern consistently.

The saying goes, "you don't have to floss all of your teeth, just the ones you want to keep."

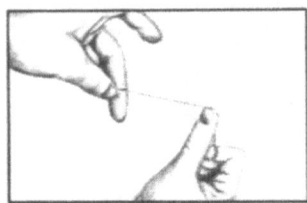

1. Wind most of 12 to 24 inches of floss around one middle finger.

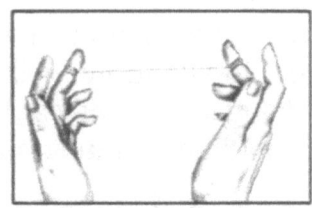

2. Wind the rest around the middle finger of the other hand.

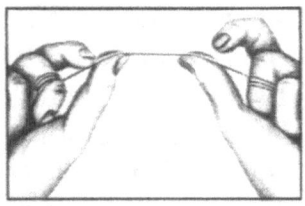

3. Floss, wrapped around middle fingers—allowing about one inch to work with.

4. Insert floss between teeth with gentle sawing motion.

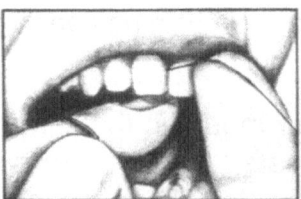

5. Curve floss into C shape around tooth at the gum line.

6. Scrape the floss up and down—repeat for all sides of every tooth.

Flossing

DIET

Sugar in your diet causes the bacteria in plaque to become more active. The bacteria digest the sugar and put out the waste products that cause disease. Sugary in-between snacks, like cookies, cakes, candies, and ice cream should be restricted. Eat these as desserts with your meals. Since the teeth are being exposed to sugars in the meal, following with a sweet dessert won't harm them much more. For snacks, eat nuts, carrots, celery and other foods not containing sugar. Avoid dried fruits, and candies, chewing gum (with sugar), and soft drinks (with sugar).

So, to prevent dental disease, eat well-balanced meals and avoid sugary snacks; take fluoride from birth and throughout life; floss at least once a day and brush twice; see your dentist twice a year for cleaning and checkups. Healthy teeth, a nice smile, and good breath will be your life-long reward.

CLEANING

A professional cleaning does more than just take the stains off your teeth. The hygienist's main task is to remove the tartar (calculus) from below and above the gums, so that the tissues can heal and remain healthy. Calculus forms when plaque is left on the teeth. As the bacteria in the plaque die, they absorb calcium from your blood and saliva. This supports the forming of new plaque, which is more difficult to remove by toothbrush or dental floss. These deposits build up layers on the teeth that are rough. This is why they must be removed from time to time by your dental hygienist. Polishing makes the teeth smoother; a smooth surface is easier to keep clean than a rough one.

How often should cleaning be done? Some people have severe gum problems that require cleaning as often as four to six times per year. Others have fewer problems and should have cleanings every six months; this is good for most of us. Still others who floss daily and have few if any problems can go a year between cleanings. Insurance will most often pay for two cleanings a year. If you need more you may have to pay for the extra appointments. However, if this is what it takes to save your teeth, it is well worth it. Trust your dentist's advice as to how often you need your teeth cleaned.

X-Rays

X-rays, in general, must be used with caution. No one should be subjected to more x-rays than needed. Because of improvements in x-ray equipment and film, today's dental office uses as little as 8 percent of the x-ray that it used to take to expose a film. That means we are receiving less than 10 percent of the x-rays that we got only 20 years ago, per film.

Some people refuse to have dental x-rays at all. They believe that if they have a problem with their teeth, they will feel it. Unfortunately, this is not the case. It is common to see people come into a dental office with decay so bad that only the roots of the tooth are left. When asked if they had felt anything (other than a gaping hole where the crown once was) they say no. Abscesses are sometimes discovered that the person could not feel. So decay, bone loss, and sometimes abscesses can only be detected by x-ray.

How much is enough? That depends on the individual. People who have a great deal of decay will need x-rays more often than people who have little problem with decay. Usually two to four checkup (bitewing) x-rays once a year are enough to pick up cavities while they are small, and to watch the bone level. A full series or panoramic x-ray is a good idea every 5 to 10 years. Your dentist should know what is best for you. If you think you are being given too many x-rays, see another dentist for a second opinion.

SOME COMMON DENTAL PROBLEMS

Thermal Sensitivity. Sensitivity to hot and cold is one of the most common complaints heard in a dental office. Cold drinks, ice cream, salads, even tap water will cause some discomfort. Hot coffee, tea, and other drinks as well as food will cause some people to complain. Often that person thinks they have a cavity. Usually, the culprit is an exposed root structure. Roots are not covered with enamel but a substance called cementum. As we age, it is common for our gums to recede away from the crown of the tooth, exposing previously covered root structure. This root structure is often sensitive to heat and cold. Poor brushing technique and lack of flossing can make this situation much worse. So, what can we do about it?

The easiest and cheapest treatment for sensitive roots is to use a desensitizing toothpaste. There are several of these available in most drug stores and some grocery stores. Try using one of these for two or three weeks. If there isn't any change after using the toothpaste for this period of time, or if the sensitivity is extreme, see your dentist. He or she has several ways to treat sensitivity, the most extreme being a filling or a crowning of the suspected tooth/teeth.

Sinus Toothache. The roots of the upper (maxillary) teeth are embedded deep in the upper jaw. Some of the molar, premolar and cuspid roots go up into the sinuses. Sinus infections can put pressure on these roots, causing a toothache. If your upper teeth ache but you can't tell which tooth in particular hurts, and if you have a sinus infection or head cold, taking an antihistamine or cold tablet will sometimes relieve the pain. If you take an antihistamine and the pain continues, see your dentist as soon as possible.

Pregnancy. We have all heard the old saying "Lose a tooth with every child." Fortunately, this no longer has to be the case. Women experience many changes in their bodies brought on by pregnancy. This is a particularly bad time to neglect your body in any way. Your mouth is no exception. Proper oral hygiene is even more important during pregnancy.

The hormones released by your body during pregnancy affect the soft tissues of your mouth. These changes appear very early in the pregnancy and may at times be observed by your dentist, even before confirmation by a pregnancy test. Inflamed gums are more common, and more severe at this time. Women often complain of bleeding and tender gums. There is also a local swelling that may develop in the gums commonly called a "pregnancy tumor." These are not usually severe, and usually disappear after pregnancy and nursing.

The developing baby gets first priority from the woman's body. Calcium is rapidly taken up by the baby's growing bones and muscles. This is one reason why obstetricians usually prescribe a calcium supplement along with vitamins for expectant mothers. If there is a shortage, it will show up in the mother, not the baby.

In our discussion of gum disease, it was noted that the gums become inflamed and the supporting bone of the socket is attacked by the inflammation and gradually destroyed. Pregnancy may increase the tendency for and the rate of this disease. In extreme cases, the teeth may loosen and possibly be lost.

To be sure that none of the above problems occur, we simply must take better care of our mouths. Pregnant women should see their dentist regularly. X-rays in the first three months should be avoided except for emergencies.

The growing fetus is undergoing rapid cellular changes in the first three months of pregnancy, the different cells developing into different organs.

X-rays may cause changes in developing cells, called mutations. This is most likely to occur during this first trimester of pregnancy. This is why avoiding x-rays to the abdominal area during this time is advisable. Many dentists will not x-ray at all during pregnancy. Others feel that using a lead apron to cover the woman after the first trimester is safe.

Brushing and flossing should be done faithfully to prevent gum disease from progressing. At no time is this more important than during pregnancy, since you are more susceptible to gum disease than at any other time. Your toothbrush and dental floss are your best allies against gum problems.

A WORD ON TOOTH COLOR

Surface stains that build up on teeth are usually removed during cleaning. Most stains are caused by age, tobacco, tea or coffee, which respond better to bleaching in general. Other types of stains can be caused by antibiotics (such as tetracycline) or too much fluoride, and bleaching results are less favorable. Side effects are minimal but may cause some sensitivity and gum irritation, so any whitening procedure should be discussed in detail with your dentist. Also keep in mind that tooth colored fillings and/or crowns will not lighten, and bleaching before placement of restorations is recommended.

In-office or "laser" bleaching, at-home kits, and whitening toothpastes available over the counter are among the more popular cosmetic dentistry options and are reasonably affordable. Two other options that are more aggressive and costly are bonding and/or porcelain veneers. Again, discuss with your dentist which option is most favorable for you.

To get a better idea about how other people see your teeth, stand back from your mirror 4 to 7 feet, then smile; this is where most people see you. You will see a dramatic difference in your tooth color and general appearance than when you look at them 2 inches from the mirror. After this experiment, you will probably relax about how your teeth look.

BACK CARE

MINIMIZING YOUR RISK OF BACKACHE, AN UNNECESSARY CONDITION

G. Sevelius, M.D.

Physical pain is not a simple affair of an impulse, traveling at a fixed rate, along a nerve. It is the result of a conflict between a stimulus and the whole individual.

Rene Leriche
Surgery of Pain

Introduction

The last two chapters of this book contain information originally written for the safety of the workers in the workplace, the care of a healthy back and healthy hearing. Medical problems of the back and hearing are so common in the public that I felt the information could be useful for anybody, and therefore included the text here. The work that we do should not threaten our safety, but instead should be a positive experience that enhances our lives. The goal is to make the workplace as safe and pleasant as possible. It is my hope that the information about work safety will be a step toward that goal.

HISTORY

Lower back pain was probably first described by the Egyptians more than 5,000 years ago. In the late 1600s, Bernadino Ramazzini, the father of occupational medicine, wrote about it. Theory has it that back pain started when the human species, through evolution, changed from walking on four legs to walking on two legs. This is an appealingly simple explanation to back pain, but doesn't offer much hope for improvement. It's questionable whether mankind would have evolved to its present domination of the world if the problem was as common in the past as it is now. Back pain is actually on the increase in our society. Let's therefore examine how the back is designed to work and what we do or don't do in our daily habits to cause the back ailments that afflict so many of us. Perhaps back problems, some of the most painful of ailments, are really another category of "unnecessary" diseases!

STATISTICS

Eighty to 90 percent of the total population will be affected by back problems sometime during adult life. Most episodes of back pain occur between the ages of 20 and 50, a time when people are employed and are most productive. Back injury is by far the most common work injury. Of total sick leave used by employees, 90 percent is for injuries or illnesses that are not work related. Back pain is one of the most common reasons for missing work, second only to the common cold. The dollar cost of lost time from both work-related and non work-related back pain is unknown, but must be enormous.

ANATOMY

An anonymous writer described the spine as "a series of bones running down your back. You sit on one end of it and your head sits on the other."

The spine consists of 24 round blocks of bone, or vertebrae: 7 neck, 12 chest, and 5 lumbar. These vertebrae are stacked on top of each other, the smallest on top, the largest on bottom. The bottom block, the fifth lumbar vertebra, rests on the back portion (sacrum) of the pelvic ring (a ring of large bones). A jelly-like ball (nucleus pulposus) is located between each body of vertebrae. This ball is wrapped in a rubber-like ring (the annulus fibrosus). Together they form the disc. The rubber-like ring keeps the jelly-like ball pushed up slightly so the vertebral bodies can twist and bounce. This is how the vertebral bodies move against each other.

A ring of bone is attached to the back of each vertebral body. As the bodies stack up on top of on another, with a disc between each of them, these rings form a canal housing the spinal cord. The spinal cord is a long appendix of the brain containing both nerves from the brain and nerves of its own. The spinal cord sends out "spinal nerves" between each bone ring, one to the right and one to the left of each vertebral body. The spinal cord does not reach to the bottom of the spinal canal, but the nerves do. The lower spinal nerves reach down from the tip of the spinal cord like a long horsetail (the cauda equina).

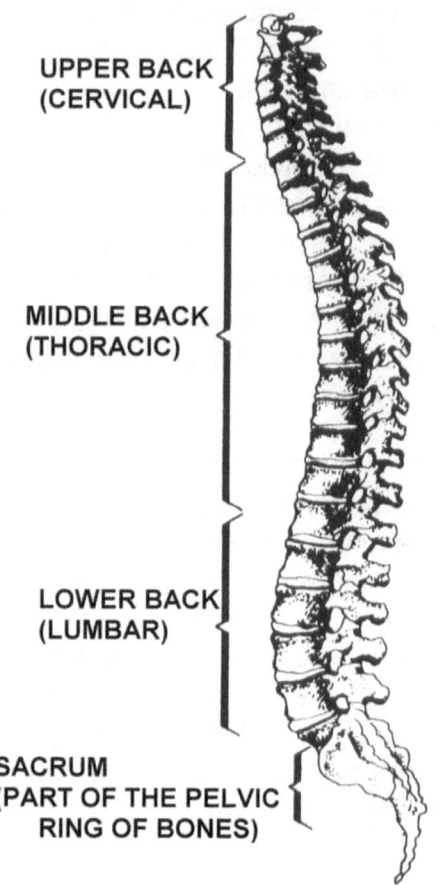

UPPER BACK
(CERVICAL)

MIDDLE BACK
(THORACIC)

LOWER BACK
(LUMBAR)

SACRUM
(PART OF THE PELVIC
RING OF BONES)

Human Spine, Viewed from Left Side

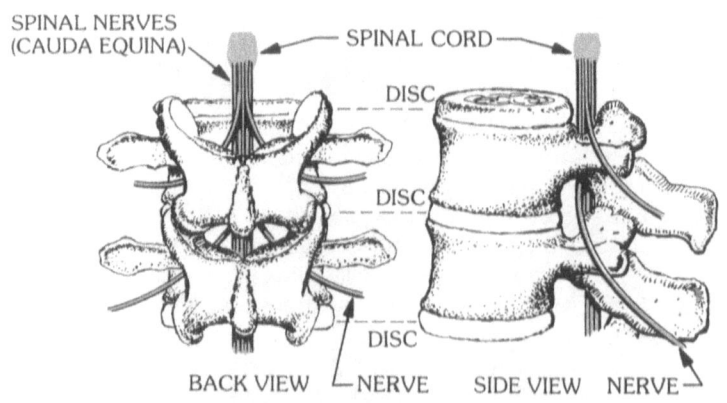

SPINAL NERVES
(CAUDA EQUINA)

SPINAL CORD

DISC

DISC

DISC

BACK VIEW   NERVE   SIDE VIEW   NERVE

**Lumbar Vertebrae, Showing Nerve
and Spinal Cord Passages**

The individual fibers reach out through the intervertebral spaces between the lower bone rings.

Each spinal nerve contains nerve fibers with ingoing impulses (afferent sensory fibers) going to the brain, and fibers with outgoing impulses (efferent motor fibers) going mostly to the muscles. The ingoing impulses travel in different nerve fibers, one for each type of sensation: touch, temperature, pain, and the position of a limb. An impulse from the skin, like a bite from a mosquito, is carried by afferent pain fibers to the spinal cord and relayed to the consciousness in the brain. Here, efferent motor nerves are stimulated to engage muscles, we hope, fast enough to swat the mosquito. Sometimes we jump because of an impulse without even thinking about it. This is called a reflex. Reflex impulses are relayed right in the spinal cord without the intervention of the brain.

Each bone ring of a vertebra (vertebral arch) has several bone processes that stabilize the vertebra. Each ring has a pair of foot-like processes on its right and left sides that rest on similar shoulder-like processes from the ring below. Each one of these upper and lower joint processes has a regular joint between them, held together with ligaments just like any other joint in the body. There are three more processes protruding from the rings, one on each side stretching sideways (the transverse process), and one in the middle stretching backwards (the spinal process). The spinal processes are the bony bumps you can feel in the back, along the spine. The transverse and the spinal processes serve as anchor points and leverages for strong ligaments and back muscles. The front and the sides of the vertebral bodies are held together by other large ligaments, which resemble heavy canvas tape.

The spine and its ligaments act as a flexible rod standing on the back portion of the large pelvic bone ring. The lower portion (the lumbar) leans slightly inward to the line of body gravity. Structural analysis of the spine, along with its ligaments and muscles, reveals that its critical breaking point is only 4.5

pounds, not enough to even hold up the head. The strength of the spine depends instead on a barrel or "tent" of muscles rigged like guy wires all around the tent-pole, the spine. The cavity of the barrel is held open by the bell-shaped ribcage that hangs and hinges on the chest vertebrae. The arms hinge from the shoulder blades at the top of the spine on the outside of the ribcage. The shoulder blades are held in place by muscles and ligaments, and are stabilized in front by the collarbones. The ribcage, being part of the barrel, is held in place by both abdominal and back muscles inserted into the ribcage, spine, and pelvic bone ring. When lifting something with the arms, all the muscles surrounding the spine and the thoracic and abdominal cavities contract, turning the cavities into supporting "air-splints" for the spine itself. The pressure from the arms and shoulders is thereby spread, not just to the spine, but to the whole pelvic bone ring.

The barrel theory for the stability of the spine has been verified by measuring the actual pressure, in different body positions, on the jelly-like ball of the discs between the lower vertebral bodies. The pressure is lowest when we are lying down. The pressure is increased when we stand. The highest pressure, however, is when we sit unsupported. This is when abdominal muscles are relaxed, the line of gravity falls in front of the spine, and the weight of the upper body is concentrated on the spine with no weight distributed over the floor of the pelvic ring.

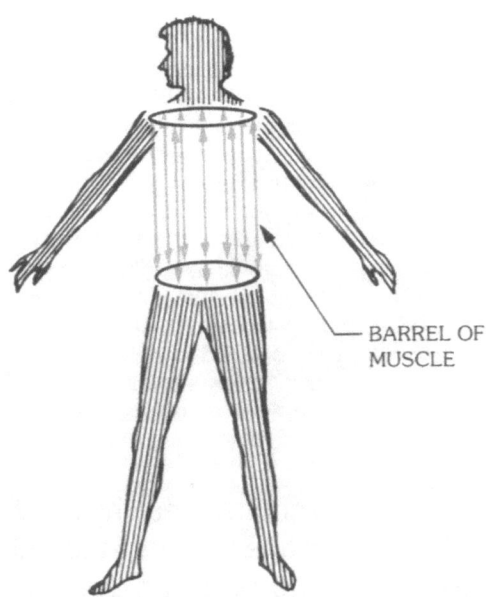

BARREL OF
MUSCLE

**Barrel or Tent of Muscle Supports
Spine's Upright Position**

The barrel theory explains the importance of keeping the full ring of muscles all around the spine in good shape to avoid backache. When any portion of this tent is weak, failure of the spine may occur. Backache, for instance, is the most common medical complication astronauts suffer after returning from the weightlessness of space (where there certainly is no heavy lifting). Our culture tends to induce weaknesses in the front portion of the barrel much more so than in the back. The abdominal portion of the tent tends to get weak from two common modern problems, prolonged sitting and excess weight. Nibbling potato chips in front of the TV for hours might cause the viewers of a sports event to have a higher incidence of backache than the participants in the sport.

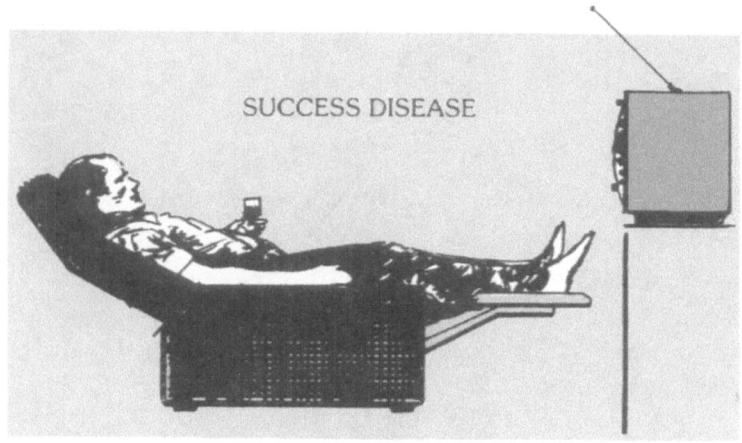

SUCCESS DISEASE

Backache in the Making

Each part of the spine has a critical breaking point. The weakest point is the lower back, because it carries the most weight with the least leverage. When the breaking point is reached, the first parts to break are the muscles, then the ligaments, later the rubberlike ring around the jelly-like ball in the disc, and last, the bodies of the vertebrae. The total strength of the spine is related to size, gender, and age. Taller people are, in general, stronger than shorter; males are stronger than females; and younger people are stronger than older. There is, however, great individual variance, dependent on personal habits. There is a close correlation between all muscle groups of an individual (unless he is scarred from injury or malformation). A strong handgrip is therefore, in general, indicative of strong muscle support for the spine. This is mentioned because a test for handgrip may be used to test the strength of a person's back.

PAIN

The sensation of pain is a very complicated process, still not fully understood by medical science. Pain is started by the stimulation of the particular nerve fiber transmitting pain. Pain impulses enter the spinal cord through the spinal nerves and are then relayed to the brain and the consciousness. The severity of the pain, as we perceive it, is related to our past experiences. For most people such experiences are related to sports or other intense physical activities from our youth. Many women compare a severe pain to childbearing experience. Still, severe pain for one individual may be only moderate pain for another.

Another factor that affects pain perception is the secretion of a hormone-like substance, endorphins, in the brain. Endorphins may block the perception of pain in the brain. The secretion of endorphins is increased by physical activity, so athletes tend to have higher amounts. It is believed by some that acupuncture can stimulate the secretion of endorphins.

A third factor that influences the experience of pain is the "placebo effect." This is the effect, real or not, that belief has on the experience of pain. It has been estimated that 50 to 70 percent of all pain can be influenced by a placebo (an inactive sugar pill).

These "subjective" variables make treatment of pain a real art. Many clinics are now specializing in the treatment of intractable pain, much of it severe, longstanding back pain. It is interesting to note that most of these pain clinics don't use pain medications, but work on the psychological experience—the brain image of pain.

BACK STRAIN

The most common back injury is lumbar back strain. This strain can be due to an excessively strong effort, a very sudden effort, or an unusual effort. The symptoms are lower lumbar backache and tenderness. The lumbar muscles on each side of the lower spine are usually soft and relaxed, despite their tenderness. Usually the pain does not radiate into the legs or buttocks and the treatment can be simple rest and heat. Many sportsmen use treatments of icepacks for 20 minutes, three times per day. While the muscles are anesthetized from the ice, the back is exercised first by passive, then by active exercise. The passive exercise consists of lying on the back, lifting the pelvis by pulling in the stomach while someone lifts the legs. Soon the back is actively exercised by lifting the legs on their own to "work the pain away." Diagnosis of back strain is established by clinical examination; x-rays of the back and pain medications are usually not necessary.

BACK SPRAIN

Back sprain, a slight tear in the tissues, is a more severe injury to the muscles and ligaments of the spine. Symptoms may include a slight slippage of vertebral bodies relative to each other, so the arches or their ligaments may press on or irritate the spinal nerves; swollen and tender back muscles clinched in a spasm that will not allow any movement of the spine; and local pain in. the lumbar back. There may be pain radiating down into the buttocks and the legs on one or both sides. Acute pain can be relieved with local cold packs, but it is wise to treat a back sprain with total bed rest. Aching, tense muscles can be relieved with local heat and muscle-relaxing medication, including anti-inflammatory pain medications such as Naprosyn, Motrin, and others. Slight pain relief can be achieved with pain medications, but total relief is difficult to accomplish without the risk of overdosing the medications. In most instances, the spasm will be relieved in a few days. Diagnosis of back sprain is determined by clinical examination. X-rays of the spine may be required to exclude more serious injuries.

RUPTURE OF THE DISC

A disc may rupture because a heavy lifting load puts pressure on the jelly-like ball in the middle, straining the surrounding ring to the breaking point. This usually only happens under extreme circumstances. More common is the breaking of the ring after a moderate strain, preceded by uneven wear on the rubberlike ring due to poor posture or malformation of the spine at birth. This causes the jelly-like ball inside the ring to be pushed out through the weak part of the ring. The break usually occurs on the backside of the disc, more or less to one side, thereby pushing on one of the spinal nerves. This is called a herniated disc. It causes intense pain in the back and in the area that this nerve serves, as in a leg or a buttock. Disc herniations occur most often between the lowest lumbar vertebra and the back of the pelvic ring (sacrum) because this area carries the heaviest load and has the most flexibility.

The diagnosis of which spinal nerve is being affected can be determined by how far down the leg the pain reaches. Regular back x-rays do not reveal the jelly-like ball or the disc but may show a displacement of a vertebra. The most common way to establish the exact location of the herniated disc is to inject an x-ray opaque fluid into the spinal canal. The herniation of the jelly-like ball will show on x-rays as a filling defect of the x-ray fluid. This procedure is called myelography. It can be a painful and occasionally dangerous procedure and should not be done unless surgery is contemplated, or tumors or other more unusual diagnoses need to be excluded.

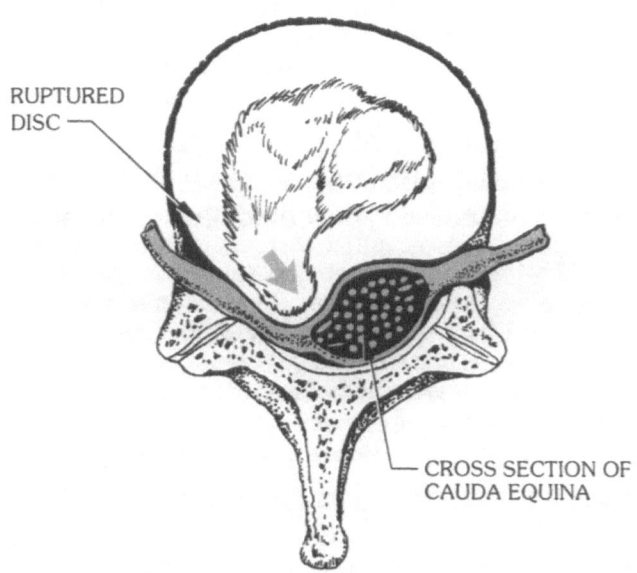

RUPTURED
DISC

CROSS SECTION OF
CAUDA EQUINA

Schematic Cross Section Showing

Compression of Nerve Root

Another procedure for the diagnosis of a herniated disc is to obtain an image of the spine with a computerized axial tomography (CAT) scanner. This is a painless procedure and does not require an injection.

The treatment of a herniated disc with typical signs of spinal nerve compression involves, at first, six weeks of bed rest. This allows a possible over-diagnosed sprain or minor tear in the disc a chance for spontaneous healing. Statistics show that 98 percent of all back pains are caused by self-healing injuries and heal, sooner or later, by conservative measures.

If symptoms are not improved in six weeks, surgery should be contemplated if a herniated disc is positively identified. In surgery, a window in the ligaments is made between the spinal arches, and the herniated portion of the disc is removed. Some surgeons cover the scarred arches with bone grafts to make the spine more stable (spinal fusion). Full recovery from surgery can take several months, but most people are back to work in about six weeks.

The Food and Drug Administration (FDA) recently approved a drug that can be injected to dissolve the herniated disc. Such a procedure eliminates the trauma of major surgery. The new drug is a papaya extract called chymopapain. One problem with the drug is that it might dissolve nerve tissue if accidentally injected into a spinal nerve. This could lead to paralysis, but so far this has been a rare complication.

THE EFFECT OF AGE
ON THE BACK

Normal aging affects all four elements of the back: the disc, the ligaments, the muscles, and the bones. The disc tends to decrease in size as we age because the jelly-like ball dries up and the surrounding ring wears down. The ligaments tend to stiffen, and the muscles of the back—the total supporting muscle tent around the spine—get weaker from the more sedentary lifestyle of advancing age. The spaces between the vertebral bodies tend to fill up with bone growth and bone spurs when they are not being used. In medical terms, this is called degenerative arthritis of the spine. Lack of movement will further decalcify the vertebral bodies and eventually they may collapse from lack of calcium. Such a condition is called osteoporosis. This usually only happens in very advanced age. Degeneration of the spine comes from inactivity, and the only way to avoid it is to exercise the spine with stretching motions even when the body feels stiff. It will always take an effort to fight off the stiffness that comes with age.

BACKACHE AND SMOKERS

Two very interesting recent medical reports relate smoking to backache. Doctor Nachemson's team in Gothenberg showed that smoking diminishes the flow of nutrients to the discs, and Dr. Trymoyer, et al., showed in population studies that backache was more common among smokers.

PREVENTION OF BACKACHE

Because backache is the most common work injury, much effort has been spent on its prevention. The greatest success has been with ergonomics, the science that seeks to adapt working conditions to the worker. Medical examinations are less successful particularly attempts to select a worker for a specific job on the basis of an x-ray of his lumbar spine. Statistics show that individual variations of spinal vertebrae are of little consequence for the future risk of back injury. Recent statistics from firefighters in Los Angeles are even more revealing. The lack of back injuries related more to general cardiovascular fitness than to the strength of the back. The firefighters who were cardiovascularly unfit had ten times more back injuries than those in good cardiovascular condition. Cardiovascular fitness was the main factor in preventing back injury. Therefore, an accurate medical selection for a heavy lifting job should include evaluation of anatomical build, strength, and cardiovascular fitness. Cardiovascular fitness is determined by checking the resting pulse rate or the change in pulse rate during exercise. A slow resting pulse rate and a slow change to a work demand indicates greater fitness.

**Exercise for Workers Who Must Sit
for Extended Periods of Time**

Many back injuries happen to office workers who spend much of their time sitting and are only occasionally required to lift something heavy. Three to four-hour periods of sitting wither away the strength of the abdominal muscles, leading to weak support for the back during lifting. Realizing this fact, modern Japanese factories have stretching breaks. There is considerable theoretical evidence that this will lessen chances for back injury in a work situation.

A worker who depends on back strength for a livelihood must care for his back as a piano player cares for his hands. The worker should follow these suggestions:

- Stay in good cardiovascular condition and never allow resting pulse rate to exceed 72 beats per minute.
- Maintain proper weight and never exceed 20 percent overweight.
- Don't smoke.
- Consider back-strengthening exercises as a way of life and do 20 push ups and stretching exercises each day to keep your abdominal muscles tight, joints open, and ligaments and muscles limber.

- Consider taking up aerobic exercise to promote blood flow and delay bone degeneration and early aging.

LIFTING TECHNIQUES

With proper knowledge of the anatomy and physiology of the spine, we can now find a proper lifting technique for each situation.

When faced with a lifting job, size up the job first. Ask yourself, "Is the job too big for me to handle alone? Should I ask for help?" If not, sizing up the challenge will allow time for reflexes to mobilize and adrenalin to shift blood to flow to your muscles so they will be physiologically prepared for the challenge.

Before you start your lift, check the passage to the unloading area to see if it is free from obstacles.

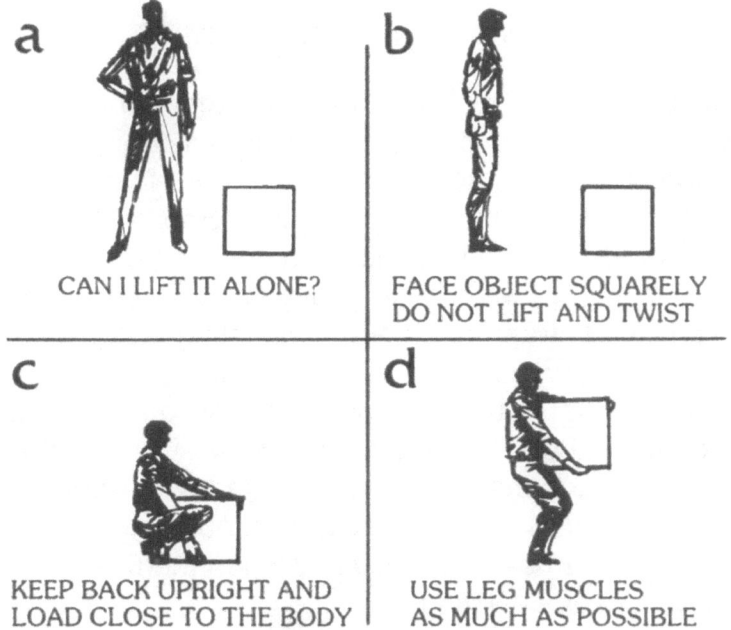

Lifting Techniques

Avoid twisting the body while lifting. Twisting will disengage a portion of the muscle tent, immediately exposing the spine to possible strain or sprain.

If a load has to be carried, always hold it close to the body to avoid unnecessarily heavy leverage on the back.

If something has to be lifted from a low shelf or floor, bend the knees, not the back, when reaching down. Keep the back as upright as possible, giving the spine support from its total muscle tent. If necessary, use a shoulder strap to reach down around the object and raise it, again with a straight back, while using the legs to lift.

If two people are lifting, be clear on your signals so that one does not let go and the other is suddenly left holding all the weight.

KNOW YOUR LIFTING LIMITS

In most people, the grip will fail just before the maximum safe lifting strength of the back is reached. Because of this correlation, it is helpful to know the strength of your handgrip. This can be determined with an instrument known as a dynamometer, available in most doctors' offices. No lifting work should involve weights so heavy that they challenge your maximum lifting strength. In fact, most lifting tasks should not exceed half of your maximum lifting strength. This approximate limit corresponds to the recommendations published by the International Labour Organization. However, with the help of the grip dynamometer, estimates of back strength can be more individualized. In critical situations, actual testing of back strength might be useful, particularly when medical conditions might preclude heavy lifting.

If heavy loads like tools are to be handled by many different employees, mark the weight directly on the tools so that co-workers will know what weight they are asked to lift. If possible, don't store heavy tools above shoulder level or below knee level. Rapid, repetitive lifting tasks should only be done with loads that can be handled by arm strength alone, the back being engaged only to support an upright body position. Repetitive lifting jobs that require stooping can probably be improved by proper ergonomic engineering.

For a more in-depth treatment of proper lifting techniques on the job, see the appendix.

Name: _____

My grip strength (equals the maximum weight I am capable of lifting):	☐
The maximum recommended weight for me to lift (when in proper position):	☐
The maximum recommended weight for me to lift during repeated lifting (rate = one lift per minute):	☐

STANDING

Standing requires work by the total muscle tent of the spine. Like all muscles, the tent fatigues less if allowed to contract and relax at intervals—promoting blood circulation. Moving about a little while standing will prevent fatigue when standing for a long time. Most people find it comfortable to stand with one leg raised on a low stool so that the pelvic ring is raised slightly in front, thus creating a flat platform for the lumbar spine.

**Leg Position for Workers Who Must Stand
for Extended Periods of Time**

Standing for long periods places strain not only on the lumbar back but also on the arches of the feet. Workers who are required to stand a lot should wear sturdy shoes with solid arch support.

Standing also promotes pooling of blood in the lower legs, which might lead to varicose veins in the legs. Sturdy shoes, elastic stockings, or walking in place will counteract pooling of blood.

SITTING

Sitting for long periods can be very demanding on the lumbar back because the back is deprived of support from the abdominal muscles. This support has to be compensated for by well-placed back and arm support from a chair. Again, as with standing, most people benefit from a slight upward tilt of the pelvis, which can be gained by placing the feet on a footstool, sitting close to the wheel while driving, pulling the knees up against the front seat in an airplane, or sitting with crossed legs. Sitting for many hours on international flights can be very tiring, so break the monotony by walking around. This will avoid pooling of blood in the feet and fatigue of the back.

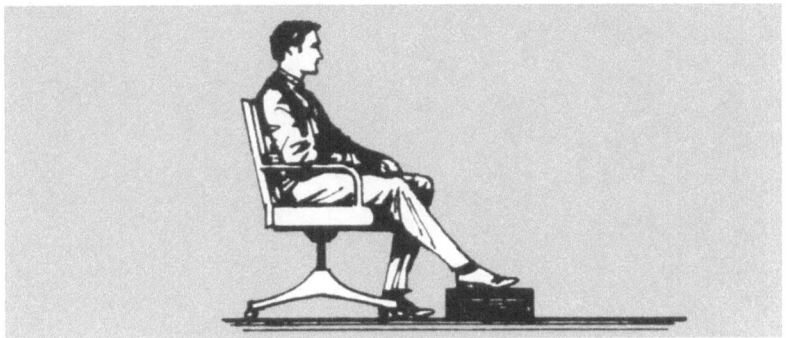

Leg Position for Workers Who Sit

SUMMARY

The spine is an elastic rod that stands on the pelvic ring. It is held up by a tent of muscles around it. To avoid a back injury when engaged in any major lifting effort:

- Size up the job; get help if it's more than 80 percent of your maximum lifting strength or if the load is physically difficult to handle.
- Lift with both hands while holding the load close to your body.
- Lift with your legs while holding the back straight.
- Avoid twisting while lifting.
- Maintain normal body weight, good cardio-vascular fitness, and good musculoskeletal fitness especially good abdominal muscle strength through daily exercise.
- Don't smoke.

Gunnar G. Sevelius, M.D.

Keeping physically fit and using proper lifting techniques will help you avoid one of the most common medical ills, the backache.

It will add years to your life and life to your years.

APPENDIX

LIFTING ON THE JOB

There have been many attempts to estimate a weight that is safe for most people to handle. These attempts have not been very successful, however, because only about one third of back injuries are directly related to a strong lifting effort. Most work- related back injuries are the result of hoisting or jerking a load, slipping while carrying an object, and so on. Still, the risk of injuring your back when lifting a very heavy object is three times greater than normal because you have to use your maximum effort to handle it.

The International Labour Organization (ILO) proposed safe lifting standards, adjusted for the age and sex of the worker. Table 1 gives the suggested weight limits proposed by the ILO.

Table 1. ILO Suggested Limits for Occasional Weightlifting

Age (Years)	Men (kg)	(lbs)	Women (kg)	(lbs)
14 - 16	15	32	10	22
16 - 18	19	41	12	26
18 - 20	23	50	14	30
20 - 35	25	54	15	32
35 - 50	21	45	13	28
Over 50	16	34	10	22

kg = kilograms

The strength required for a certain lift depends on the level the load has to be lifted from, how far out from the body the grip is, and how often the lift has to be performed. Figure 1 gives some idea of how the strength required to lift an object is modified by such factors.

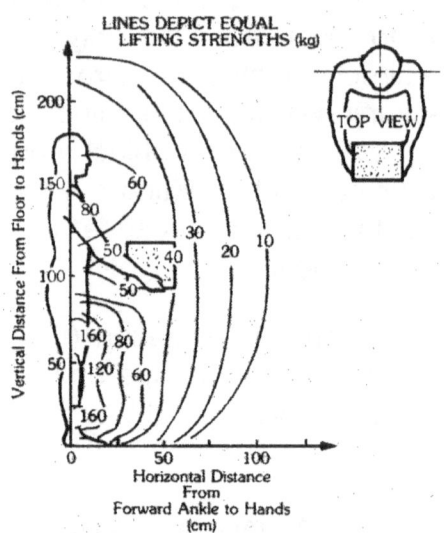

Figure 1. Predicted Lifting Strength of Large/Strong Male
(Reprinted from the *Practice Guide for Manual Lifting*,
NIOSH Publication 81-122)

The National Institute of Safety and Health (NIOSH) published a *Practice Guide for Manual Lifting* (NIOSH Publication 81-122). The maximum weights acceptable to male and female industrial workers (adjusted for one lift per minute) are listed in Table 2.

**Table 2. Maximum Weights Acceptable to Male
and Female Industrial Workers**

Height of Lift	Sex	Mean (kg)	(lbs)	Standard Deviation (kg)	(lbs)
Floor to knuckle	Male	28	62	8	17
	Female	17	37	3	7
Floor to shoulder	Male	23	51	6	12
	Female	14	31	3	7
Floor to reach	Male	22	49	5	11
	Female	13	28	2	5
Knuckle to shoulder	Male	26	57	7	15
	Female	15	32	3	7
Knuckle to reach	Male	24	53	5	11
	Female	12	26	2	5
Shoulder to reach	Male	20	44	5	10
	Female	12	26	2	4

kg = kilograms

Figure 2 shows three regions and boundaries defined for infrequent lifting from the floor to knuckle height. Depending on the size of the object and the location of the hands, the maximum weight that can be lifted can be determined.

Gunnar G. Sevelius, M.D.

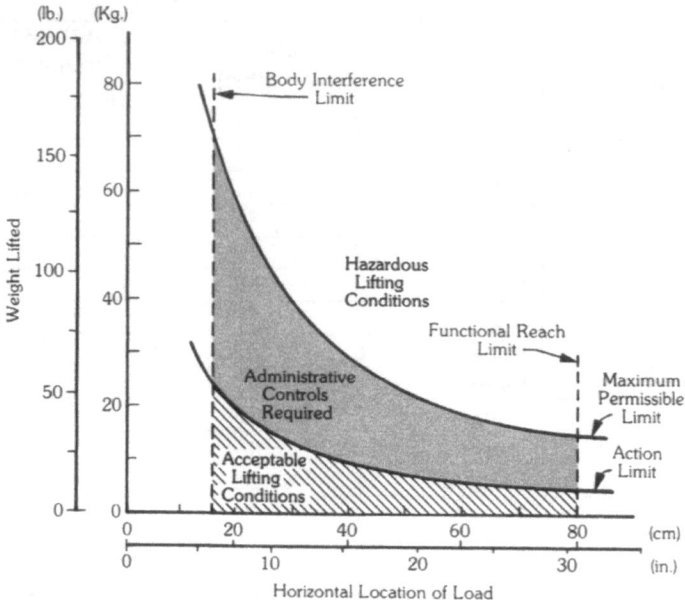

**Figure 2. Maximum Weight vs. Horizontal Location for Infrequent
Lifts from Floor to Knuckle Height**

180

NOISE AND
HEARING CONSERVATION

G. Sevelius, M.D.

Nature has given man one tongue, but two ears, that we may hear twice as much as we speak.

Epictetus (about 50-130 A.D.)

INTRODUCTION

The purpose here is twofold: to explain how noise in the industrial environment may affect an individual, and to demonstrate hearing conservation methods and their importance.

The body has five senses: sight, smell, taste, touch and hearing. To lose hearing is to miss a lot of what's going on in the world around you. Hearing loss from noise creeps up gradually over the months and years until, when you finally notice that you don't hear well any more, it's already too late. Don't let that happen to you.

Even a partial hearing loss will affect your ability to get along in social situations. You'll have trouble following the group conversations and you may make mistakes because you didn't hear something right. You'll have more difficulty hearing people with soft voices, such as children, and you can't hear music as well.

The best remedy is prevention through an effective hearing conservation program, in which manage-ment and labor must work together. The major elements of an effective program are:

- Noise exposure measurement
- Audiometric (hearing) testing
- Hearing protection
- Education
- Engineering controls

DEFINITION OF SOUND

Sound is a vibration in a medium, usually air, that produces the sensation of hearing by affecting the human ear. The sound waves vary in how quickly they vibrate (frequency) and in height (amplitude). The different frequencies give the different pitches of the sound; the higher the frequency, the higher the pitch. Frequencies are measured in cycles per second, or Hertz, abbreviated Hz. The human ear can register only those frequencies between 20 and 20,000 Hz. Higher frequencies, which the human ear cannot hear are called ultrasound. The size or amplitude of a sound wave creates the loudness of the sound. It expresses the energy or the pressure of the sound wave. The pressure is measured in units called decibels (dB). Zero decibels is defined as the lowest sound that can be heard by the human ear. The ear is particularly sensitive to sound in the middle frequencies, between 500 and 2000 Hz. The following table lists noise levels of some common sources.

Some Common Noise Sources and Levels

Noise Source	Decibels (dB)
Jet engine	140
Riveting on steel tank	130
Cutting machine-hardened tools	120
Pneumatic hammer	110
Pneumatic drill	100
Shouting heard a few feet away	90
	80
	70
Voice, normal conversation	60
	50
	40
Very soft whisper	30
	20
	10
Threshold of human hearing	0

DEFINITION OF NOISE

In its broadest sense, noise is either an unpleasant sound or a sound that interferes with one's ability to hear what one *wants* to hear. From an industrial medical standpoint, noise is a sound that may cause hearing loss, whether or not it is music to our ears.

NOISE MEASUREMENT

Noise exposures in the workplace are normally measured by the industrial hygienists who are responsible for administering the company's hearing conservation program. The hygienists determine whether or not workers should be included in such a program, and how much noise reduction is needed from hearing protectors. Noise measurement is also a necessary first step when engineering controls are to be installed. Noise exposure is usually measured with an ordinary sound level meter.

Some sound level meters have three scales or "weighting networks," labeled A, B and C. The A scale is used most frequently because it best reflects the sensitivity of the human ear to different sound frequencies. Measurements using the A scale are sometimes referred to as "dBA." The C scale is often used for determining the attenuation (noise reduction) values of hearing protectors. C-scale measurements are referred to as "dBC."

Figure 3. Noise Dosimeter

Sometimes, when employees move around quite a bit or when noise levels fluctuate, use of a noise dosimeter works out well. This little instrument, illustrated in Figure 3, takes measurements automatically throughout the work shift. The microphone, which is worn on the collar or on the shoulder, picks up the sound and transmits it to a device like a tiny computer, which is worn in the pocket. Because the microphone is somewhat sensitive, it is best not to bump it, or to talk or blow into it.

ANATOMY OF THE HUMAN EAR

To understand how sound may cause hearing loss it becomes necessary to understand the anatomy of the ear and how it works. The human ear consists of three main parts: the outer, the middle, and the inner ear (see Figure 4). The outer ear, which consists of skin and cartilage, collects the sound waves and directs them through the ear canal where they strike and vibrate the eardrum. On the other side of the eardrum is the middle ear. It consists of three small bones linked together, the hammer, the anvil and the stirrup. The first bone, the hammer, is attached to the relatively large eardrum. The hammer rests on the anvil, which in turn is linked to the stirrup. The third bone, the stirrup, is attached to a very small drum which leads to the inner ear. The purpose of this bone linkage, from a large to a small drum, is to enlarge and modify the sound wave before it is transmitted to the inner ear.

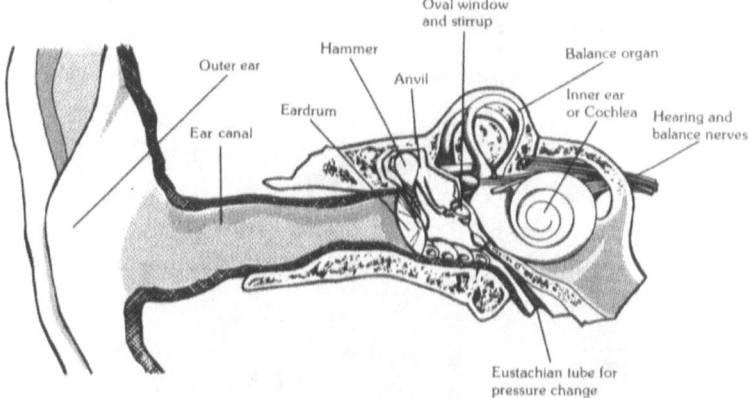

Figure 4. Anatomy of the Ear

The middle ear is exposed to air pressure changes: from the outside of the ear via the ear canal and from the inside of the middle ear via another canal, the eustachian tube. This design allows pressure to equalize on each side of the eardrum, a common sensation when we fly.

As illustrated in Figure 5, the inner ear resembles the shell of a snail and is called "cochlea." The cochlea is totally imbedded in the base of the head bone. Inside the bony cochlea is the hearing organ, the "Organ of Corti." It consists of a coiled membrane that goes the entire length of the snail-shaped structure. Situated on the membrane are small sensory cells with tiny hairs at their tips. The tiny hairs touch a small overhang or roof, and the entire unit is submerged in a viscous body fluid. Depending on their location along the membrane, different "hair cells" respond to different sound frequencies. The ones near the apex (top) of the cochlea are sensitive to low-pitched tones and the ones near the base (closest to the outside world) are sensitive to high-pitched tones.

When a sound wave enters the ear it causes the eardrum to vibrate. The vibration is passed along by the hammer, anvil, and stirrup into the cochlea, where it causes the fluid in the organ of Corti to vibrate. The vibrating fluid causes the hair cells to bend, which activates a nerve impulse. The nerve impulse is transmitted to the brain as an experience of a certain sound. This process repeats itself millions of times a day in what we take for granted as "hearing."

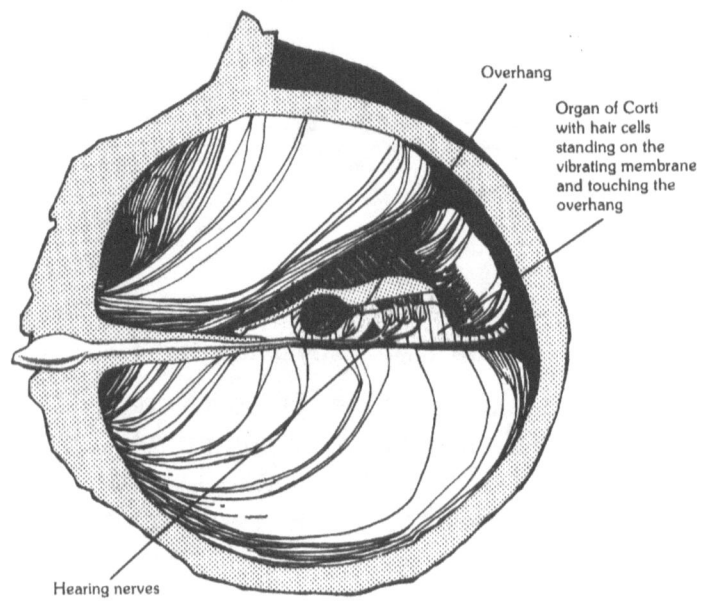

Overhang

Organ of Corti
with hair cells
standing on the
vibrating membrane
and touching the
overhang

Hearing nerves

Figure 5. Inner Ear

The hearing organ, due to its microscopic size and intricate design, is extremely sensitive. Once destroyed it can never be totally replaced or repaired. Sudden extreme pressure waves can tear the outer eardrum, or derange the small bones of the middle ear. Prolonged exposure to loud noise tends to destroy the hair cells in the Organ of Corti. Some degree of hearing loss is natural with age; the hair cells simply wear out through the years. This is called presbycusis, which to some degree, affects everyone. Presbycusis commonly affects the ability to hear high-frequency sounds. For example, an elderly person is often unable to hear the ring of a telephone. It is not precisely known whether this loss is solely due to aging or if it is combined with a loss due to the constant noise surrounding most people in a modern society. Loss of hearing from "normal" society noise is called socioacusis and would include damage from such sounds as loud music, power tools, and prolonged exposure to traffic noise.

Noise levels in most factories are anywhere from 60 to 120 dBA. Although industrial noise contains mostly low and middle-frequency sounds, the ear is most sensitive in the high-frequency hearing range (about 2000 to 6000 Hz). Noise-induced hearing loss almost always occurs first and most severely at 4000 Hz, and to a slightly lesser degree at the other audiometric frequencies close by, such as 3000 and 6000 Hz. A hearing loss for these high-frequency sounds often makes it difficult to understand speech, particularly the high-pitched consonant sounds. In the English language, the consonants (for example p, d, t and s) rather than the vowels (for example a, e and o) tend to carry the message of a sentence. If one were to leave out the vowels in the phrase "consonants carry the message," the remaining meaning is still discernible, c-ns-n-nts c-rr- th-m-ss-g-. The same is not true if one were to leave out the consonants, -o—o—a— -a—y —e -e—a-e. The loss of the ability to hear the consonants of the alphabet therefore is a drastic limitation on a person's ability to communicate. As a person begins to lose his hearing, typically, he will first be unable to hear plurals; he is unable to hear the "s" at the end of the words. As the hearing worsens, words will sound like grunts, "pass the sugar" may sound like "-a-u-uga." The person will be aware of the conversation, but will be unable to discern what is being said. These hearing changes can and usually do occur very slowly and many people may at the beginning not be aware that they have a hearing problem.

Here are some early signs of hearing loss:

- Temporary but lingering loss of hearing after short periods of exposure to high noise levels.

- Inability to hear and understand conversation in a noisy environment.

- Family members commenting on one's inability to hear.

- Head noises, particularly ringing or buzzing in the ears (tinnitus).

HOW TO UNDERSTAND YOUR AUDIOGRAM

When your hearing is tested in an audiobooth, you will be asked to listen to some tones, most of which will be very soft (Figure 6). Usually the tones are given at frequencies of 500, 1000, 2000, 3000, 4000 and 6000 Hz. The weakest tones you can hear are called threshold values. These are recorded on an "audiogram." A young person with normal hearing should be able to hear at or under 10 dB at each frequency.

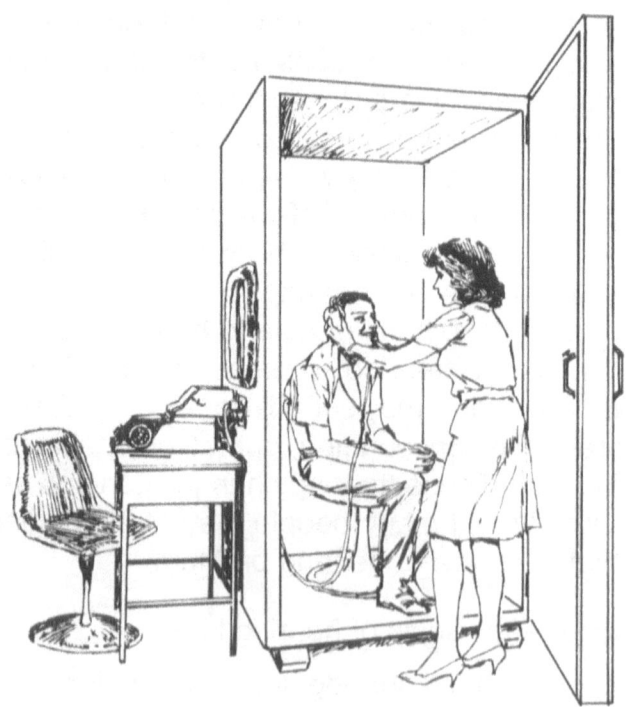

Figure 6. Audiobooth

Progressively, after the age of 30 or 40, one normally loses some hearing ability and will have higher threshold values, especially at the 4000 and 6000-Hz frequencies. It is normal for hearing thresholds to vary somewhat from test to test. Deviations of less than 5 dB from one year to the next are acceptable due to audiometric variations. Yearly deviations greater than 10 dB should, however, be evaluated further. The first audiogram with a company (the baseline audiogram) is compared to each annual audiogram. If the hearing thresholds on the annual audiogram have shifted by as much as 10 dB average at 2000, 3000 and 4000 Hz, the shift is called a "significant" or "standard" threshold shift, and certain precautions need to be taken.

The first step in evaluation is always to retest, checking the calibrations of the instruments, and checking the patient. Has the hearing rested sufficiently? (At least 14 hours away from loud noise exposure.) Has there been any wax buildup, cold or allergy? If the threshold shift persists, it should be evaluated both from a medical viewpoint and from an industrial safety viewpoint to establish a plan for corrective measures, and very importantly, the hearing protection needs to be checked. Perhaps the size is incorrect or maybe the protector is not being inserted properly.

In the following graphs you will see some samples of audiograms. An audiogram is a graph that shows a person's ability to hear controlled sounds produced by an audiometer. Frequency is given along the horizontal side and intensity is given on the vertical side, with the larger numbers representing greater intensity and thus greater hearing loss. Standard symbols are used to record a person's hearing ability, with Os used to record right ear hearing levels and Xs used to record left ear hearing levels.

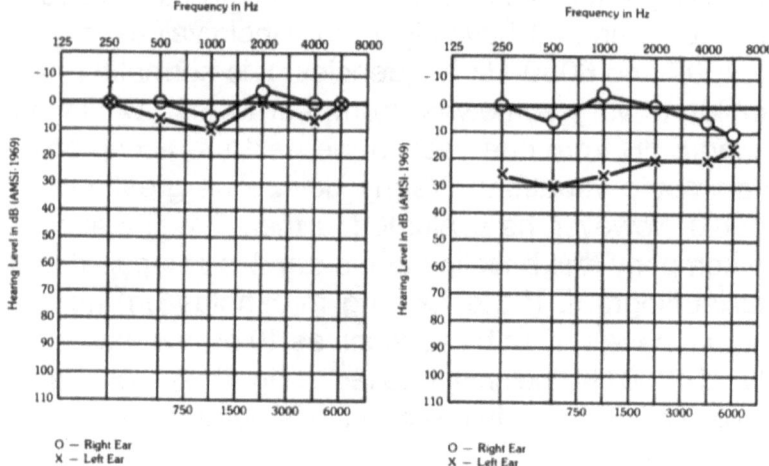

O — Right Ear
X — Left Ear

O — Right Ear
X — Left Ear

This audiogram shows completely normal hearing. The right ear is even a little better than the left ear.

This audiogram shows a mild, "flat" type of hearing in the left ear. This picture is typical of impacted wax or perhaps an ear infection in the left ear. The condition is usually medically treatable.

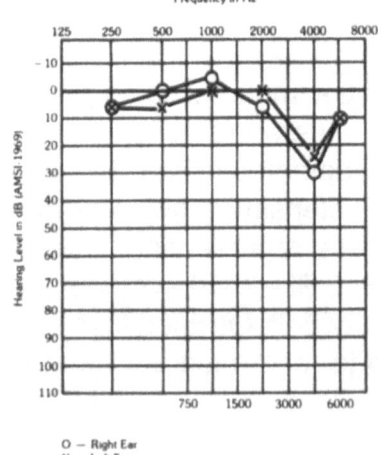

O — Right Ear
X — Left Ear

This audiogram shows a mild decrease in hearing ability at the 4000-Hz frequency. It may have been caused by noise. This person is probably not yet aware of the hearing loss.

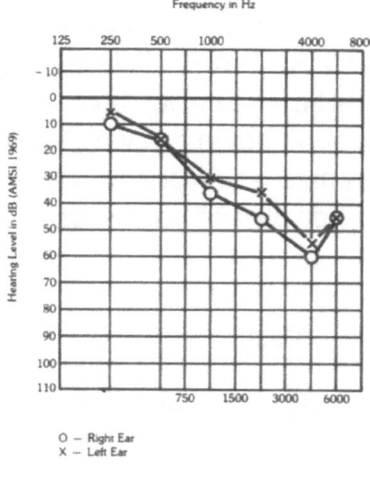

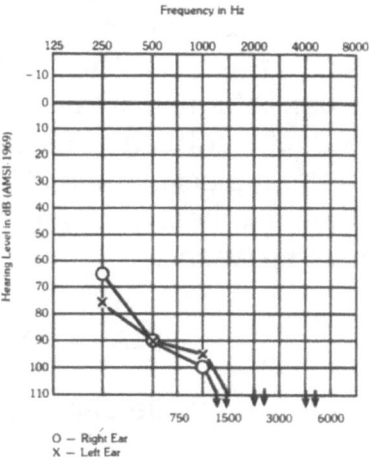

This audiogram shows a moderate hearing loss that is severe in the high frequencies. This person would have difficulty understanding speech, especially in a noisy background. This condition is typical of many years of exposure to loud noise.

This person is deaf. The arrows indicate no re-sponse to sound in the high frequencies. This con-dition is not characteristic of noise exposure. It is most likely hereditary or caused by a childhood disease.

MINOR EAR MALADIES

Minor ear problems usually can be treated with home remedies, while others require a physician's attention. Healthy ears are particularly important when earplugs are to be used.

EAR WAX

Ear wax is produced by special glands in the ear canal. The wax glands are located in the outer part of the canal, where there is also some hair growth. The purpose of the wax is to keep the hair sticky in order to trap foreign particles such as sand and dust and prevent them from entering the ear canal. Normally this wax will accumulate and then migrate to the outside where it dries and falls away. If one should have an over abundance of ear wax, consult medical personnel who may offer to wash it out or remove it with special instruments. It is not advisable to try to do this yourself because the skin of the ear canal and the eardrum are extremely fragile and can be injured easily. Since wax is formed in the outer part of the canal, probing with cotton swabs or bobby pins might pack down the wax towards the eardrum blocking sound transmission or possibly injuring the drum. It is best to clean the outer part of your ears with a warm damp washcloth.

EARS AND ALTITUDE

The air in the middle ear is constantly being absorbed in the body. Air is resupplied through the eustachian tube during swallowing. This enables the pressure on both sides of the eardrum to remain equal. When the pressure is not equal, the ear feels blocked. Rapid changes in air pressure may occur during air travel. This is especially true when an airplane is either ascending or descending. The change from a low pressure (high altitude) to a high pressure (low altitude) causes a vacuum to form in the middle ear. Even though modern planes have pressurized cabins, there are still some pressure changes. To help equalize the pressure in the ears one may need to swallow frequently. This opens the eustachian tube and allows air to pass into the middle ear and equalize the air pressure. If one has a common cold or is suffering from an allergic condition the eustachian tube may be blocked due to swelling of the membranes. If this is the case, taking some decongestive tablets before the trip is recommended. These will reduce the swelling in the membranes.

SWIMMER'S EAR

Swimmer's ear is an infection· of the outer ear canal caused by a fungus, mold or other common bacteria. After swimming, moisture and body heat create a perfect environment for fungus or bacteria to grow causing infection in the ear canal. Infections may be prevented by washing the ear canal with an eyedropper filled with alcohol and household vinegar after swimming. This solution will help the water to evaporate and kill bacteria and fungus.

Ear Itch

Ear itch can be caused by a fungus, but often it may be due to a noninfectious irritation, such as an allergic eczema. Both skin and wax become dry and flaky. Ear drops containing cortisone administered three times daily may help relieve this problem. If the condition persists you should consult a physician.

Foreign Objects and Insects

Gnats, moths and roaches are the most common types of insects that can get into the ear canal. Gnats can easily be washed out with warm water from a bulb syringe. For large insects, fill the ear with mineral oil. This will seal off the breathing pores of the insect and kill it. It takes about five to ten minutes. A physician should then remove the insect. Some common objects that children put into their ears are beads, pencil lead, erasers, and pieces of toys. Removal should be left to a physician so as not to cause any damage to the ear.

Safe Noise Limits

There are limits to the amount of noise a person may be exposed to on the job. Most companies with noisy operations have hearing conservation programs to prevent exposure to hazardous noise levels. For added safety, the Occupational Safety & Health Administration (OSHA) has recently adopted hearing conservation requirements which will apply to everyone.

All sound levels from 80 to 130 dB must be monitored and figured into an employee noise exposure rating called the 8-hour Time Weighted Average (TWA). The maximum safe exposure for the normal or average individual is considered to be a noise dose equivalent to 8 hours of continuous noise at 90 dB. The dose

Gunnar G. Sevelius, M.D.

is calculated from the relationships between actual exposure times at each level and the permissible exposure times for those levels shown.

Permissible Noise Exposures	
Duration Per Day (Hours)	Sound Level dBA Slow Response
8	90
6	92
4	95
3	97
2	100
1-1/2	102
1	105
1/2	110
1/4 or less	115

When an employee's calculated noise dose, as measured by an industrial hygienist, is 85 dB or more, that employee should be given yearly audiometric exams, instruction about hearing conservation, and hearing protection. Hearing protection must be worn when the 8-hour TWA exceeds 90 dB. Of course, it is preferable to reduce the noise levels by engineering efforts, but that is not always feasible.

HEARING PROTECTORS

One method of protecting our hearing from excess noise is by wearing hearing protectors. If these devices are carefully selected and fitted, they can reduce the noise level at the eardrum by as much as 20 to 30 dB. There are a variety of hearing protectors available. The most commonly used are earplugs and ear muffs. (The type of hearing protector used will vary according to the policy of the individual company. Protectors should be issued at the time instruction is given about hearing conservation and hearing protection.)

EARPLUGS

Earplugs are small devices made out of rubberized plastic, polymer foam, or other nontoxic materials (Figure 7). To achieve proper noise reduction, plugs must be fitted tightly into the ear canal. If the rubberized plastic type is used, the wearer should reach around the back of his head with the hand opposite the ear to be fitted, and pull the ear out slightly. This process straightens the ear canal so that the plug is easily inserted. If the foam type is used, the foam cylinder should be rolled between the thumb and forefinger until it looks like a golf tee. Then, you insert the rolled-up end in the ear, press it, and hold it in firmly for about a minute while it expands to fill the ear canal.

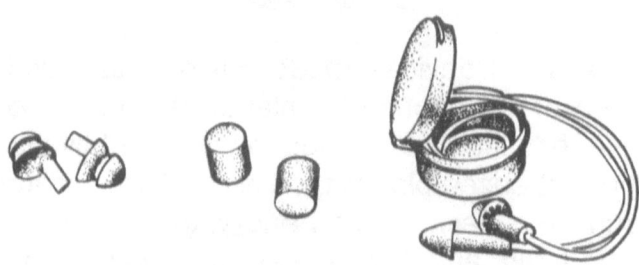

Figure 7. Three Kinds of Earplugs

Earplugs have many advantages. Because they are small, they can be worn in confined spaces. They are lightweight and can be worn comfortably all day. They are not appropriate in conditions where they have to be removed often, especially when workers have chemicals, dirt, or grease on their hands. Earplugs should always be inserted with clean hands.

EARMUFFS

Earmuffs consist of plastic cups containing sound attenuating materials, attached with a headband (Figure 8). The headband can be worn under the chin, or behind the head as well as over the head. Some muffs are attached to safety helmets.

Earmuffs are easier to fit than earplugs, but care must still be taken to ensure that the ear cup and headband are the right size. The cup should fit all the way around the ear and the seal between the cushion and the head must be continuous. Plastic safety glasses or even clumps of hair should not come between the cushion and the head.

Figure 8. Earmuffs

CARE AND MAINTENANCE OF HEARING PROTECTORS

Like any piece of equipment, hearing protectors have to be cared for. Earplugs should be washed regularly with soap and water. Even some of the "disposable" plugs, such as the foam cylinders, can be reused it they are washed. Plugs should be dry when they are reinserted. Earmuff cushions should be wiped with a damp cloth. Care should be taken not to "spring" (loosen) the earmuff headband, otherwise the muff will no longer be effective.

Hearing protectors eventually wear out. Disposable types will wear out quickly, but the others can last for months or even years, depending on the usage. Plugs may eventually shrink or become brittle and lose their effectiveness. Muffs may become loose or the cushions may lose their springiness. If your protectors show signs of wearing out, you should obtain a new pair from the organization who issued the original protectors.

Gunnar G. Sevelius, M.D.

GETTING USED TO
HEARING PROTECTORS

People in high-noise environments who first start to wear hearing protectors usually report that they feel better right away. They notice that they are less tired and irritable, and that they sleep better at night. Sometimes people who work in moderately noisy environments have some difficulty adjusting to the protectors because the improvements are not quite as dramatic. New hearing protectors may be somewhat uncomfortable at first, and require a period of adjustment. But if you continue to experience discomfort after a few hours, return them to the issuing organization for a different protector.

SUMMARY

Noise exposure greater than the permitted 90-dBA TWA, if allowed for extended periods of time, can be a hazard to our ability to hear in later life. The company will provide baseline audiograms and annual audiometric tests to every worker who spends most of his or her working time in an area where the average sound level is 85 dBA or greater. A shift in the audiogram of 10 dB or more should be examined from a medical and an industrial safety viewpoint. Noise may be controlled by engineering modifications or by the use of personal hearing protection devices. Earplugs and earmuffs are the most commonly used. All of these devices should be treated with great respect and cared for properly, making sure that they are clean and most importantly that they are used.

ADVICE TO THE SUPERVISOR
CONTROLLING NOISE AT THE SOURCE

The most effective way to control noise is to engineer it away. The design stage is the most important time to consider the noise level that equipment will generate. Reduction of noise at the source is a problem that management, designers, supervisors, foremen and operators can all help to solve. Noise level also should be a factor to consider in selecting and purchasing new machinery.

Some simple engineering measures may be implemented to decrease noise from machines already installed. Noisy machines may need greasing, balancing, a noise-isolating platform, or possibly simply isolation. There are many ways to decrease noise. Some practical suggestions are listed below:

Distance or Relocation. Distance reduces noise levels from a point source by 6 dBA per each doubling of the distance in a free field. (This rarely occurs indoors.)

Vibration Control or Isolation. The control of vibration is vital for a quiet work environment. To achieve this, mountings should be made of springs, rubber, cork, felt, or fiberglass.

Damping. *This procedure involves the addition of layers of vibration absorbing materials to either side of vibrating surface.*

Lagging. This procedure is used in pipes and other surfaces radiating noise by covering them with one to four inches of acoustical material that is covered with heavy shielding such as seed filled vinyl, or other metal protective coverings.

Air and Gas Flow Noise Reduction. Absorptive silencers contain porous materials to absorb and reduce noise. Reactive silencers depend on reflection of the sound waves. Both types are used depending upon the design of the machine.

Gunnar G. Sevelius, M.D.

Air Jet Flow. The turbulence caused by high-velocity airflow machinery can be a tremendous noise source. Low noise level jets are available and can be tested to see if they do the job. If the jet is from a vent, it may be vented outside the operating area or muffled. Air operated tools should have exhaust mufflers.

Hydraulic Systems. Gear pumps are noisier than screw pumps. The noise level increases with the speed of the pump. Hydraulic mufflers may be used to lower the noise level. Fluid flow lines that have sharp bends cause turbulence, which cause vibrations and noise. If it is not economical to change the design of the pumps, other methods can be used to reduce noise, such as lagging or using elastic spacers and flexible pipes.

Motor Air Noise. This noise can be reduced by acoustic line airflow chambers. Totally enclosed fan cooled motors are also available.

Enclosed Drives. The vibrating surfaces can be damped to reduce noise, or quieter drives can be substituted which use belts for gears and silent chains for roller chains.

Noise Source Enclosures. This reduces the localized noise source, such as metal-to-metal contact areas of a machine. Where the machine cannot be enclosed, it may be possible to enclose the operator.

CALCULATING ALLOWABLE NOISE LEVELS

Noise varies over a work shift in most factories; under such circumstances noise exposure is calculated as a "time-weighted average" sound level according to the formula:

Daily dose = $C_1/T_1 + C_2/T_2 + C_3/T_3 + C_n/T_n$

where C is the total time at a specified noise level and T is the allowable time at that level.

The maximum allowable steady-state noise level is 115 dBA, regardless of any computed time-weighted average. Impulse noises, such as explosions, riveting, or loud hammering, should not exceed 140 dB (peak sound pressure level). For purposes of the hearing conservation amendment, impulse noise should be integrated into the daily dose. A dosimeter is the most convenient method of doing this.

An employee exposed to a time-weighted average noise level of 85 dBA or more during his work shift should have a baseline audiometric test at the beginning of his employment and every year thereafter, unless there are other medical circumstances calling for more frequent testing.

WARNING SIGNS

Any area requiring hearing protection (greater than 90 dBA) should be posted with a warning sign. Keep in mind that OSHA requires workers who have experienced a "standard" threshold shift to wear hearing protection over 85 dBA.

```
WARNING

HIGH NOISE AREA

MAY CAUSE HEARING LOSS

USE PROPER EAR PROTECTION
```